SWIMMING IN THE SINK

Lynne Cox

———

SWIMMING IN THE SINK

An Episode of the Heart

To Marilynn —
all the best wishes
with your open water
swims! Go Gauchos!
Lynne Cox

ALFRED A. KNOPF   NEW YORK   2016

THIS IS A BORZOI BOOK PUBLISHED BY ALFRED A. KNOPF

www.aaknopf.com

Knopf, Borzoi Books, and the colophon are registered trademarks of
Penguin Random House LLC.

Names: Cox, Lynne, [date]
Title: Swimming in the sink / Lynne Cox.
Description: First [United States/American] Edition. | New York :
Alfred A. Knopf, 2016.
Identifiers: LCCN 2015041418 | ISBN 9781101947623
(Hardcover : alk. paper) | ISBN 9781101971833
(Trade Paperback : alk. paper) | ISBN 9781101947630 (ebook)
Subjects: LCSH: Cox, Lynne, [date]- | Swimmers—United States—
Biography.
Classification: LCC GV838.C69 A3 2016 | DDC 797.2/1092—dc23
LC record available at http://lccn.loc.gov/2015041418

Jacket illustration by Ben Wiseman
Jacket design by Janet Hansen

Manufactured in the United States of America
First Edition

To Dave and Beth Yudovin

One beat separates life from death, silence from music, waves from shore.

Contents

SWIMMING IN THE SINK

1

THE BUCKET

I thought it would be easy to immerse my hand in a bucket of thirty-two-degree Fahrenheit water (zero degrees centigrade). I swam across the Bering Strait wearing a swimsuit in thirty-eight-degree Fahrenheit water (three degrees centigrade). I swam for two hours and six minutes and reached Russian shores. The water temperature in the bucket was only six degrees colder than the Bering Strait, but my hand ached. It was shouting at me to lift it out.

I was jet-lagged and sitting wearing a swimsuit in a laboratory at the University of London. Dr. William Keatinge, one of the world's experts on the effects of cold on the human body, had asked me to participate in the study. He was measuring blood flow into and out of my hand in the cold. The goals of his studies were to contribute to medical research and learn more about how people survive in cold water.

There were monitoring devices attached to me: thermocouples on the fingers of my left hand, forehead, and right toe measuring my skin temperature. I had a rectal probe—a thin wire inserted in my body—measuring my core temperature.

Dr. Keatinge was standing near the monitoring devices with two researchers. They were watching the screens, and Dr. Mattie Scarborough, an internist, was sitting beside me to make sure I was okay.

I focused on the pace clock in front of me. The clock had two hands. The red hand was the second hand and the black hand was the minute hand. The red hand seemed to be moving slowly. It seemed like the seconds were minutes. I didn't think I would be so uncomfortable. I tried to focus on my breathing. My breathing was fast. I was anxious. I never knew what to expect when I was asked to participate in research tests. I should have known it would be challenging. These tests always were. I knew how to train for channel swims and I knew how to adapt to unexpected situations, but these tests were different. I had to push myself mentally and physically in ways I had never done. I never knew what would happen or what the outcome would be. It was exciting to explore with the researchers, and learn things we didn't know, but it was also challenging, and sometimes frightening.

How could six degrees Fahrenheit make that much difference? I thought my hand would adjust to the cold and it would relax; that's what happened when I swam in cold water. But my hand felt different in the bucket. It felt as if it were freezing to an ice tray. The pain made me queasy.

Dr. Keatinge warned me that the test could be difficult. He had run other tests on me, and he had accompanied me on my Bering Strait and Beagle Channel swims. These were swims that hadn't been done before. He was on the support boat to observe me and make sure I didn't go into hypothermia and die. Dr. Keatinge thought that I was very different from other people he studied. He was right.

From the moment I was born, my parents knew I was different. I was born almost a month early. My parents were worried. They weren't sure I would survive. My body was covered with fine, soft, wooly hair. My mom said that I looked like a little seal. They had never seen a baby covered with downy hair. It was a sign for them that I was going to be different. They worried when I was born because I weighed only five pounds. But I quickly put on weight, and I grew larger and much stronger than other children my age. I think it was a survival mechanism that kicked in.

My parents now worried that I was larger than other children, and my dad, who was a radiologist, had me tested. The pediatrician discovered that I have an efficient metabolism, which helped me thrive and become an endurance athlete. My parents encouraged me to swim, and I discovered that I loved being in the water more than on land.

I was lucky; at an early age I discovered something I would always love. I was lucky, too, because my parents always supported me and gave me a lot of freedom.

When I was only six years old, they let me visit the neighbors on my own. The neighbors were from all over the globe. I was intrigued by their differences, because I was different too. They told me stories about their childhoods and why they decided to come to America. They told me America was a special place where they could live their dreams while continuing to celebrate their cultures. They brought the art, food, and music from their homelands. Knowing them enriched my world and made me realize that being different was good.

My dad said that the color of one's skin is only a wrapping. It doesn't matter. Everyone is human. Everyone needs to be cared for. My mom was an artist. She loved to paint pictures of people with different skin colors and physical characteristics. She said their differences made them beautiful. I realized that it was the differences among us that made life fascinating.

My neighbors liked me because I was different. Mrs. Smith said I was patient and determined. She liked me to visit her, and we had tea and cookies with her three orange cats and Heidi, her huge German shepherd with large white fangs.

Heidi had long shiny brown and tan fur and large brown eyes. She looked so soft and beautiful and I wanted to pet her, but Mrs. Smith said she would bite people who were not members of the family. My friends were afraid of Heidi and would never have petted her, but I thought I could find a way for her to like me. I took this on as a challenge.

One day when Beth, my Dalmatian, and I were walking past Mrs. Smith's home. Heidi ripped through the front screen door and attacked Beth, putting five large bloody punctures in her back. Beth was howling in pain as she ran home.

Heidi frightened me, but she was gentle with Mrs. Smith. She would put her head in Mrs. Smith's lap and nudge her arm with her wet black nose so Mrs. Smith would pet her.

I thought that if I was patient, Heidi would give me a chance. I visited Mrs. Smith every day, sat on her couch, and began by sticking out my index finger when Heidi walked past, so she would feel my touch. The first time I did it, she turned and glared at me. I thought she was going to bite me. But she just walked away. I was scared, but I did it again the next day, and the day after that.

I was patient. After a month I touched her with four fingers, and then one day she walked over to me and put her large head in my lap. I could feel the heat from her head, and I could feel her heart beating. Mrs. Smith said I could pet her.

Heidi had brown fur on her ears and muzzle that was so soft, and she closed her eyes when I scratched behind her ears. She was in bliss. I visited her every day after that. She walked beside me around the house, and she sometimes grabbed my hand in her mouth and asked me to pet her. But I always waited until I was sitting down and she put her head in my lap. She looked at me like she loved me. Her eyes were soft, and her mouth opened into a smile. We became friends. I learned that by being patient and persistent I could do what I wanted to do.

Sometimes Dr. Smith would come home when I was visiting his family. Dr. Smith, the oldest doctor in the neighborhood, had thin white hair and thick glasses, and he was always serious. I was a little afraid of him, but one day, I asked him if he liked cutting people open.

He seemed surprised and said he had never been asked that question. He said he didn't enjoy it, but it was what he needed to do to help people. He removed organs that were diseased or defective and repaired organs that were affected by an injury. I was fascinated by his abilities. He knew so much about life and the way the body functioned. My friends weren't interested in medicine, or in spending time talking with adults, but I was thrilled to hear his stories. I sought out the other doctors in the neighborhood to learn from them as well.

Dr. Duffy lived around the corner. He was an anesthesiologist and his daughter was my best friend. I would play with my friend and wait for him to come home after work. Dr. Duffy spoke with a slight Irish accent. He was short, bald, had bright blue eyes, and loved explaining how he put patients into a state of suspended animation so they wouldn't feel pain during surgery. I thought it was magic that he could put them to sleep so they didn't feel a thing.

Our other neighbor, Dr. Tung, was an anesthesiologist too. He studied anesthesiology in China and also did acupuncture. He explained how he inserted needles into different parts of the body to open passageways and reduce pain. It was difficult for me to imagine that sticking needles into someone's body could help relieve pain, but I believed him.

And I visited Dr. Nenopoulos. His daughter was my friend. He was an ob-gyn and he knew I was a swimmer. He told me intriguing things about life. He said that babies swam around in their mothers' stomachs in salt water for nine months. When they were born, he caught them, and then they took their first breath. He said that moment always seemed like a miracle to him, and it did to me too.

I loved learning about life and being with Arthur Daviau, my grandfather. He was a doctor and a long-distance swimmer who swam across cold-water lakes in Maine. He believed that genes had a great bearing on people's health and development. I thought I inherited my love for and acclimatization to cold-water swimming from him. He thought so too.

My grandfather was a public health doctor and he knew that there were illnesses that were genetically carried in families. His cousin, Victor McKusick, was a geneticist at Johns Hopkins University, and he agreed. My grandfather knew that people could inherit good genes too. I thought I inherited his good genes and that predisposed me to becoming a long-distance swimmer. I trained for years in cold water and I thought I was acclimated to the cold and that the cold-water immersion would be easy. But this test was the most difficult and excruciating I had ever endured.

I glanced at my hand in the bucket. It looked strange with the thermocouples attached to my fingers. My hand was ghostly white and shaped like a claw. When I swam across the Bering Strait my hands turned gray, but they never turned white.

The frigid water was shutting off blood flow to my hand. It wasn't receiving oxygen or warmth. I think the tissues were suffocating and starting to freeze. I wanted to open and close my hand to pump blood, warmth, and oxygen into it, but I wasn't supposed to move. That would interfere with the test.

Dr. Keatinge was standing near the entrance of the lab with two researchers. They were checking the monitors.

"Lynne, are you okay?" Dr. Keatinge asked. His blue eyes focused on me and his face was full of concern.

I nodded. I wasn't, but thought I would be.

He encouraged me. "We're getting good readings. They will be helpful."

I reminded myself that I was doing this for a higher purpose, to further medical research. My dad had encouraged me to participate in cold studies. He said that in the future doctors would cool patients before heart surgeries to slow body functions and after heart attacks to reduce damage to the heart and give it time to recover. Doctors would cool patients after spinal and brain injuries to reduce swelling and trauma. The tests could also help researchers figure out how to rewarm people after life-threatening cold exposure and increase their chances of survival.

The tests that were being conducted on me were already helping people. Dr. Richard Edlich, an emergency room doctor at the University of Virginia, had read Dr. Keatinge's studies and contacted me about the cold studies I was participating in at the University of California, Santa Barbara, and the University of London. Dr. Edlich had multiple sclerosis and was trying to figure out how to improve treatment for the illness. He explained that people who have multiple sclerosis often have problems with balance, maintaining muscle strength, and spasticity. Heat and cold water could exacerbate spasticity. He experienced these symptoms, but he started swimming in cold water, and that helped him regain his muscle strength and balance, and reduced his spastic episodes. He discovered that if he swam in cool water for thirty minutes or more he experienced what he called a "halo effect." After he climbed out of the swimming pool he was able to walk normally for two to three hours. He wondered if he could prolong this effect if he acclimated to lower water temperatures. But he had to make sure his core temperature didn't drop or he would shiver, his movements would become spastic, and he would have difficulty swimming and walking.

We discussed my training methods for acclimating to

cold water and he adapted my process to his workouts. After a few months, he was able to swim in cooler water, for longer periods of time, and prolong the halo effect. He shared what he learned with other researchers. It helped me to remember him while I had my hand in the bucket of ice water. I hoped Dr. Keatinge's research would provide more answers to medical questions. But it was extremely difficult to stay focused on positive thoughts.

The pain was beyond anything I had ever experienced. I told myself that if I quit, the money, time, and effort everyone had invested in the tests would be wasted. It would be embarrassing. I had to endure. I wondered how I could interrupt the pain signals to my brain and break the pain cycle.

Out of the corner of my eye, I watched Dr. Scarborough. He was leaning forward in his chair. His large brown eyes were focused on me. His brow was deeply furrowed and his lips were pursed together.

I stared at the pace clock. I couldn't believe how long it took for one second to pass. It was strange how pain changed one's perception of time. When I trained in a swimming pool and used a pace clock the seconds flew by.

I dug my nails into my right hand and hoped I could trick my brain. If my right hand hurt some, I thought it would diminish the pain in my left hand, but it didn't help.

Dr. Scarborough had asked me to call him Mattie. He had not participated in this cold-water test, but the two researchers conducting the test had. Mattie monitored the research subjects to make sure they were medically safe and consulted with the researchers. He explained that part of the protocol for conducting research on human subjects was dictated by the Nuremberg Code, a set of research ethics for human experimentation that was established as a result of the Nuremberg Trials after World War II. The code called for researchers to experience a study themselves before they tested other human subjects—and most did so. They believed it gave them a greater understanding of what the subjects were experiencing.

Dr. Keatinge couldn't participate in the cold-water study because he had Raynaud's disease, which caused blood vessels in his hands to overreact painfully to the cold. The arteries in his fingers went into vasospasm, a sudden restriction of vessels that dramatically limits blood flow. The condition was extremely painful. He said he was lucky he had a mild case. Some people lost their fingers and toes because of the disease. I wondered if his affliction motivated him to study the effects of cold on people.

Dr. Keatinge glanced at me and realized I was struggling. He knew me well. We had met when I was a student at the University of California, Santa Barbara, and Dr. Barbara Drinkwater, Dr. William McCafferty, and Dr. Steven Horvath were studying me at the Institute of Environmental Stress. During one test, I swam in 50 degree Fahrenheit water (10 degrees centigrade) for four hours and my core temperature increased from my normal temperature of 97.6 degrees Fahrenheit (36.4 degrees centigrade) to 102 degrees Fahrenheit (38.8 degrees centigrade). The researchers couldn't believe my results. When people are immersed in 50 degree Fahrenheit water (10 degrees centigrade) their core temperature drops, and the longer they stay in the water, the more their temperature drops.

The tests Dr. Drinkwater, Dr. McCafferty, and Dr. Horvath ran on me confirmed that I was in tune with my body, that I was training it to not only survive but to be stronger and excel in the cold water. I needed that confirmation. The coach I had before I entered university convinced me that I needed to swim six hours a day in a single workout in the ocean to break the world record for swimming the Catalina Channel. After those workouts, I was exhausted, too tired to sleep, and I had no appetite.

I attempted the Catalina crossing, but when I was more than halfway across the channel, and two hours ahead of the world record, I did not care. I decided I wanted to get out. I stopped swimming. For more than an hour I treaded water and argued with my crew. I told them I was burnt out. The crew concluded that there was nothing wrong with me. They convinced me to continue swimming because they thought I would regret quitting. I struggled but worked through my negativity and became the fastest person to swim the Catalina Channel.

A few days later, I decided I was done channel swimming. I was so tired of it, I couldn't look at the ocean. I told my parents I had decided to quit swimming. They said I could do whatever I wanted to do, so I visited friends, read books, and went to see movies.

A few months later, I heard the call of the ocean in the sea breeze rustling the palm trees in front of my home. I smelled the sharp notes of salt, felt the cool moist air awaken my body, and felt the pull of the tide that grew stronger as the moon grew fuller. I missed diving into clear cool blue water, the feeling of the waves lifting and embracing me. I missed the joy and strength that swimming gave me. I knew I had to return to the water, but I needed to do something different.

There were only a few people attempting long-distance open-water swims, and fewer swimming in cold water, and there weren't any coaches who specialized in open-water swimming. I realized that I knew how my body responded to stress better than a coach. While I was in college, I decided to coach myself, but I knew I needed to do something more to become faster, and stronger, and swim in colder waters. To accomplish this, I studied and spoke with world-class athletes, learned how they trained, and figured out how to translate elements of their training to open-water swimming, to my training. Their help was invaluable, but I realized I needed to do more to excel in sports and in life.

I looked at the pace clock. It was ridiculous. I could

swim across frigid oceans, but I was fighting to keep my hand in a bucket of ice water. For some reason I told myself the pain would disappear in nine minutes. My hand would be used to the water and I would be okay. I don't know why I told myself that.

I watched the black minute hand move. Nine minutes passed. I looked at my hand. It was snow white and full of pain so I glanced at kind and caring Mattie. His curly brown hair and large dark-rimmed glasses made his face look pale. There were black circles under his eyes. He looked exhausted.

One researcher asked me to lift my hand out of the water and straighten my fingers. He ran an infrared wand over my hand to measure heat flow into and out of my hand, then he asked me to put my hand back into the bucket. I wondered how long I could do it. I never knew that the more intense pain became, the more energy it took to fight it. I was trying to figure out if there was a way around the pain or a way to let go and not fight it.

Dr. Keatinge said everything was going according to plan. He left to check on some things in his office.

I looked at Mattie.

"Do you need to stop?" he asked, and grabbed a towel.

2

MIND SHIFT

I was tempted.

After a long swim, nothing feels as good as being wrapped in a warm towel. It is the reward for swimming hours in cold water and overcoming challenges. But I hadn't earned a warm towel. I hadn't completed the test. I had to endure, but I was scared.

My hand felt hard, like frozen meat, and I wondered if the ice water surrounding my hand was crystalizing my blood. My mind could override my body's response to pain to a certain point. But this was a different kind of pain than I had ever experienced.

I was searching for a mind shift—a new way of thinking that would help me escape the intense pain.

A mind shift was something that Dr. Roger Bannister, the British runner and neurologist, achieved when he broke the world record by running a mile in less than four minutes.

Before his attempt, most people believed that it was

impossible for people to break the four-minute barrier. But shortly after Bannister's success, other runners ran the mile in less than four minutes. Bannister's achievement created a mind shift. It changed the way people thought and inspired them.

My hand had been immersed for fourteen minutes and ten seconds. Each second was a tiny victory. I reminded myself that small victories lead to large ones, but my resolve was teetering. I could not concentrate. I started counting. That worked when I was tired on a long swim. But it wasn't working now. A shrill alarm was sounding in my head.

"It might distract you if I talk with you," Mattie said, and smiled reassuringly. He said he was going on holiday in a couple of weeks to anywhere he could find sunshine. The winter in England had been long, gray, rainy, and depressing. He had spent most of the year working in the hospital and cold laboratory. He was craving warmth and was considering traveling to Spain, Portugal, the South of France, Madeira, the Azores, or Italy.

It would be wonderful to visit any of those countries, I said, and for a moment I daydreamed about traveling. I told him that I loved Italy, walking the narrow, winding streets, seeing beautiful and varied architecture, watching the sunlight move across the piazzas, making the terra-cotta, cream, yellow, pink, and orange buildings glow and the rushing fountains of water sparkle. I loved the smells that came from restaurant and apartment kitchens, the delicious aromas of garlic, tomato sauce, cheese, and bread, and I loved feeling the warm sunshine on my back. Mattie said he would think about traveling to Italy.

The researcher asked me to remove my hand from the bucket. He needed to take another reading, so I lifted it and made sure not to knock the wires. I wondered if my hand would be okay after the experiment.

"You're doing quite well," he said.

I nodded. I was trying my best.

The other researcher looked at the monitor and said he hadn't gotten a good reading. His colleague repeated the test.

I wondered what would happen if he couldn't get an accurate reading. I wondered if I would have to repeat the test.

The red hand on the pace clock ticked off five seconds. I wondered if there was a limit to the time my hand could be out of the water.

"Got it this time," he said.

I submerged my hand. I couldn't believe that I was so exhausted. This experience gave me a new understanding of pain, how debilitating it was, and how difficult it was for people who had to endure it.

I tried to put my body on autopilot and disconnect my body from my mind. I did this on long swims, but I couldn't do it now.

Dr. Keatinge opened the door and jogged into the lab. He spoke to the researchers, they updated him, and he said, "You've only got ten minutes remaining."

I gritted my teeth.

He instructed, "When you reach thirty minutes, Mattie will remove the wires, but you'll need to keep the probe in. We want to take a few more temperature measurements to see if the cold blood in your hand circulates and lowers your core temperature."

I nodded. I could not speak without my voice wavering.

"The rewarming phase may be rather uncomfortable," he said.

Could it be more uncomfortable than this? I wondered.

"Okay, well done, thirty minutes. You can take your hand out," Dr. Keatinge said with relief. He checked the monitor and said, "She has minute blood flow into her hand. Less than anything we've seen." He sounded thrilled.

I stood up and felt a little dizzy.

"If you walk over to the sink, I'll run some cool water over your hand. It will make it feel better. You don't want to run warm water over it; that will hurt more," Dr. Keatinge said.

When Dr. Keatinge ran water over my hand I wanted to scream. It felt like I had stuck my hand into a hive full of stinging wasps. I pulled my hand out and put it in my armpit. I thought that this would allow it to warm up gradually, but my armpit was much warmer than the water. It hurt more. I wished I could cut my hand off and reattach it when it was warm. I shook it fast and hard. It didn't help.

"You okay?" Dr. Keatinge asked.

"Not yet. Why does it hurt so much?" I was ready to cry.

"You almost completely restricted the blood flow into your hand and it's starved for oxygen and warmth. You responded to cold dramatically differently from anyone we've ever studied. The other subjects slightly reduced blood flow into their hands and their temperatures dropped. You only allowed a minute amount of blood flow into and out of your hand and your core temperature remained normal. It's astonishing," he said.

"I thought I had a high pain tolerance, but I feel like a wimp," I said.

"You aren't at all. People who get frostbite in their hands completely shut down their blood flow and their tissues freeze. Their pain during the rewarming phase is often so intense they need morphine. We don't have narcotics in the lab, but I can give you a Tylenol."

"Will the pain diminish without meds?" I asked.

"Yes, it will," he reassured me.

"I don't need to take drugs. Is it okay if I walk in the hallway?" I thought that if I could walk I would create heat through exercise and that would warm my hand from the inside.

He said I could go wherever I wanted.

I bolted out of the lab and ran the length of the hallway. It made me feel better to move, and I hoped that would oxygenate and warm the blood more quickly, so my hand would rewarm faster. For five minutes, I jogged in the hallway. Dr. Keatinge joined me and offered medications again, but I told him I was doing better. He asked to look at my hand and said that it was turning pink. The blood flow was returning. It would feel normal soon.

He needed to return to his office and asked Mattie to walk with me.

Mattie said the initial results of the test were extraordinary. The immediate results changed the way they thought about human physiology, and I hoped they would be even more valuable in the future. He said it could take months or years to fully understand the data.

That made me feel good. I took a deep breath. I was relieved the test was over, and I never wanted to do anything like it again.

Dr. Keatinge asked if he could take a look at my hand. It was hot pink and was feeling warmer. He suggested trying the tap water again—start with cold water and slowly add warm water according to my tolerance.

We returned to the lab. I placed my hand under the tap and watched the water cascade over it and splash in the sink. In five or ten minutes my hand felt almost normal.

Dr. Keatinge said it was lunchtime. He wanted to know if I was hungry and wanted to have lunch with the research team.

I was hungry and eager to talk to the team about their work, and to learn more about them. It seemed strange to do something so intense and not even know the people I was working with other than Dr. Keatinge.

We were at Queen Mary University of London located in the East End. It was a diverse area. I had heard that there was a nearby Pakistani neighborhood. I love Indian food and had heard that Pakistani food was similar. I thought the heat and spices from the food would warm me up on the inside.

It was exciting to walk with the research team through the streets of London, across cobblestone roads. This might have been where Charles Dickens once walked. The buildings were red brick, and there were people walking past carrying colorful umbrellas with interesting patterns. They wore dark clothes and bright scarves and walked quickly.

The day was foggy and gray. It was perfect—what I imagined London would be like in winter. We passed a few Pakistani restaurants and the team agreed on one.

When we walked in we smelled curries and fresh naan bread and felt warmth moving from the kitchen to the dining area. The walls were decorated with pictures of different foods and descriptions of the dishes written in curly Urdu script and English.

The restaurant owner recognized the team and escorted us to a table, handed out menus, and in a few minutes, we were eating steamy chicken, beef, and vegetable curries, platters of tender naan, and drinking sweet bright-orange-colored mango lassis from tall glasses.

The food was spicy and the steam from the dishes released their fragrance: cardamom, ginger, turmeric, and pepper. It smelled exotic and tasted delicious. We talked a little about the cold research they were conducting, but they said it took a while to understand the test results. Sometimes it took years for researchers and physicians to apply their information, but they enjoyed exploring the physiology of the human body. It was exciting.

I asked them about the tourist spots in London, and they told me the sights I needed to see.

When we were returning to the laboratory, Dr. Keatinge said he had decided to take the afternoon off so he could show me some of London. I was so excited. We saw Royal Albert Hall, the changing of the guard at Buckingham Palace, and the King's Troop Royal Horse Artillery in Hyde Park. The horses were beautiful and the troops were regal. We stopped at the British Museum and could only see a fraction of the amazing collection.

Dr. Keatinge drove me to the outskirts of London so we could have dinner with Annette, his wife. It was like a magic carpet ride, winding through the city, past shops and historic landmarks. I was happy and relaxed, and was enjoying the chance to see the great city.

Dr. Keatinge told me that the initial results of the test were amazing. He spoke in understatements and was reserved, but for the first since we met, he couldn't contain his excitement. He said he knew the test had been difficult, but he was thankful for my participation. He asked if I would consider repeating it in a couple of days. I could take some time to decide, and I didn't have to say yes.

My results were unique, perhaps startling, and he was intrigued. To learn more he wanted to do further studies on blood flow into and out of my hand. He would need to have cannulas placed in my wrist.

A cannula is a long tube that is inserted into the body with a syringe. It is a precise pressure gauge that would measure the amount of blood flow into and out of my hand. He explained that most researchers believed that blood flow into the hand was regulated at the wrist, but their findings from the initial study led him to believe that blood flow in the hand might be regulated at the fingertips.

I don't think he had any idea what he was asking me to do—how difficult it had been for me to endure the first test.

I asked him if the test was that important.

He said my responses were different from anything he had seen before, and he thought his group might discover something new and important by doing another, more in-depth study on me.

It was difficult to think about repeating the test. I felt like I'd been through a battle, and my hand was still a little numb.

Dr. Keatinge explained that the cold had affected the nerves in my hand. It might take a couple of weeks before they regenerated.

Maybe the numbness would make me feel the ice water less. Maybe because I'd experienced the test once, I would know what to expect and it would be easier. Maybe I could do it, but I didn't like needles.

He would ask his friend and colleague, who was a cardiologist, to insert the cannulas. He was expert at it. Once they were in place, I wouldn't feel them.

I asked why cardiologists are the experts with cannulas.

"They often measure blood flow in the heart," he said.

"You don't need to put a cannula in my heart, do you?" I asked.

He considered for a moment. "That would be interesting, but we only need to look at blood flow in the hand."

"That's good," I said, relieved.

I agreed to repeat the test and convinced myself that it would be easier the second time because I knew what to expect. But I felt like there was another reason I agreed to it.

3

CANNULAS

Dr. Keatinge turned on the lights in a different room in the lab and offered a chair to me. It was 5:30 a.m. I was still jet-lagged, and tense.

Dr. Keatinge told me that the cardiologist was fitting us in between rounds. He explained the procedure the cardiologist would perform and left me in the lab as he went to get a consent form from his desk for the test.

I took slow deep breaths and cleared my mind.

Ten minutes later, Dr. Keatinge returned with the form and the cardiologist. He introduced us, but I didn't hear the cardiologist's name. He said he was originally from India and he spoke with a combination of British and Indian accents. He explained the procedure in detail, and I asked him a lot of questions. He made sure I understood. I asked him if he placed cannulas in people often and he said he did and told me how they were used in cardiac surgery.

I was fascinated but nervous. I signed the consent form and he went to work.

He sat down facing me and asked me to roll up the sleeve on my left arm.

He gently turned my arm so the palm faced up and palpated my wrist. He explained he was going to insert two cannulas, one into a vein and the second into an artery.

The room was frigid and my vein and artery responded to the cold by closing down. He couldn't insert a cannula into either.

Dr. Keatinge had anticipated this would happen. He left the room and returned with a portable space heater, plugged it in, and positioned it under my left arm.

We watched the coils turn glowing red.

I placed my arm palm down over the coils and felt it grow hot. Perspiration streamed down my cheeks.

The warmth from the heater increased the blood flow into my wrist so my veins and arteries expanded. They moved toward the surface and the blue lines bulged beneath my skin.

The cardiologist palpated them and said, "Much better," and he wrapped a tourniquet around my arm. He then stood up and spread his feet to balance himself. He seemed a little awkward. He explained that usually he inserted cannulas into people when they were in hospital beds.

I asked him if it would help if I lay down on the floor. I wanted to make this as easy as I could and get it over with. He said that would not be necessary, but he needed me to hold my hand just above the coil so my arm would stay warm.

"You ready?" he asked.

I nodded and held my breath so I wouldn't move.

He took a deep breath to prepare himself and leaned over my arm. He used a syringe to open the vein in my wrist and began slowly threading the cannula tubing into my vein. I watched with queasy fascination.

Sweat formed on his forehead and streamed down his cheeks.

He dabbed the blood that had pooled around the incision site with gauze and secured the cannula in place with white tape.

He advised me not to move my hand too much. He didn't want the cannula to bruise my vein.

The cardiologist stepped back so Dr. Keatinge could see his work.

Dr. Keatinge checked my arm. He told the cardiologist he'd done an outstanding job. He explained that it took a lot of skill and concentration to thread the cannula into the vein so fluidly.

"It's great to work with a pro," I said and smiled.

The cardiologist was sweating hard and I was too. He asked Dr. Keatinge to move the heater aside.

"You okay?" Dr. Keatinge asked.

"Yes, but do you need to put in the second cannula?" I asked. This wasn't fun.

"It's crucial to the study to measure the blood pressure into and out of the hand. But if you can't tolerate a second one, we can get by with one," Dr. Keatinge said.

"All right," I said.

The cardiologist hesitated. He wanted to be sure I was okay.

"You're doing a great job. I just don't like being stuck," I said.

"I'll do this as quickly as I can," he assured me.

"Take as much time as you need. I'm okay," I said.

He used the syringe and opened the radial artery in my wrist but could not get the cannula in. He tried and tried, and finally, on the fifth attempt, he threaded it into my artery.

I was relieved when he finished and told myself that the difficult part was over.

The cardiologist stood up, grabbed his back, and stretched it. He told me to stand up slowly so I wouldn't feel faint and instructed me to hold my left arm close to my chest and not bump anything when I walked with Dr. Keatinge to the other lab. He would meet us in about an hour to remove the cannulas.

Time will go fast, I told myself. The researchers will get what they need. I didn't feel as anxious as I did the first time. I thought, Everything will be okay.

4

THE DISCOVERY

Mattie and the two researchers were ready and waiting for us. They welcomed me back like an old friend and connected me to the wires. Mattie sat beside me. Dr. Keatinge made sure the equipment was functioning, then he left to take care of other work. Mattie explained that Dr. Keatinge didn't like to see me in pain. It bothered him.

The researchers were looking at me with frowns. Mattie spoke up.

"When we tested the other subjects, they experienced some pain. They dealt with it by pounding the table, shouting, and even cursing. If you're in pain, it's okay if you do the same. You don't have to be stoic. It might make this test easier."

"Did they do anything else to handle their pain?" I asked.

"One lad from Scotland was a theological student before he was premed. He sang religious and Scottish songs at the top of his lungs. I think he was in considerable pain. His blood flow closed down more than the other subjects. We discovered that the more our subjects closed down, the more pain they experienced. That wasn't part of the test; it's just something we noticed," he said.

"Did the Scottish lad have a nice voice?" I asked, smiling.

Mattie smiled back. "He sang nicely."

"Okay, I'll make noise if I need to."

"Ready when you are," a researcher said.

I took a deep breath and hoped that it wouldn't hurt as much as before. I immersed my left hand in the bucket, and the cold was as immediate and as intense as it was the first time.

The second hand on the pace clock was moving slowly, like the first test.

"Are you okay, Lynne?" Mattie asked.

"I am. How are you?"

"People never ask me that. I'm doing quite well," he said.

"Glad to hear it," I said and felt myself tumbling into the pain cycle. I remembered that during cold swims, I ignored the cold. I didn't think about it, so I didn't give any energy to it. I tried to do the same during the test by watching the second hand and biting my cheek. Then I tried stomping my foot. It got the researchers' attention, but the distraction didn't help at all. I realized I needed to focus on the second hand and see my progress, even if it was one second at a time.

A shiver raced up my spine. It wasn't because I was cold. It was because I realized this test was going to be as difficult as the first one, and if I went through it the way I did the first time I would experience the same amount of discomfort. I needed to change something.

"Lynne, would you like me to hold your right hand? Sometimes that helps," Mattie said.

I'd love to hold your hand, I thought. It would be a nice distraction. Instead I asked, "Do you think your hand is warmer than mine? If it is, it could affect the test results, and I don't want to repeat this test."

"Hadn't considered that. I don't think it will affect the test if I hold your hand for just a few minutes," he said.

"Are you sure?" I asked.

"I'm sure," he said.

"Okay, yes, please do that," I said.

He leaned over and held my right hand. His hand was the same temperature as mine. I was relieved. I felt myself relaxing, and then something magical happened. The pain in my left hand in the cold water was cut in half. The human connection made all the difference. This was my epiphany. This was why I repeated the test. I needed to understand that it is the human connection that helps you deal with pain. That was what I needed to learn.

I looked at the second hand on the pace clock. It seemed to be moving faster.

I looked at him. He knew there had been a change in me. I think I was breathing more normally, and my body was less tense.

The minute hand moved. Two minutes passed.

"You can hold my hand a bit longer if you'd like," he said.

"No thank you," I said, but I dreaded letting go.

When I did, the pain increased. But I felt a little calmer.

With five minutes remaining in the test, Dr. Keatinge returned to the lab and checked on me. "You're almost done," he said.

When I removed my hand from the bucket I hoped the rewarming phase wouldn't hurt as much as it did after the first test, but it did.

I told Dr. Keatinge I needed to leave the lab and jog through the hall. I thought that if I could warm my core it would warm my hand from the inside out, and the pain would diminish.

Dr. Keatinge told me to do whatever I needed to do but cautioned me to be careful with my left hand, to make sure I didn't hit anything with it. He didn't want the cannulas to slip out and damage my vein, artery, or tissues.

After jogging in the hallway for twenty minutes, my hand was warmer, and I returned to the lab and put it under cool water. Mattie and Dr. Keatinge stood beside me.

Mattie asked if I wanted to hold his hand.

I reached out and took it.

"I can't believe holding your hand makes such an enormous difference. It makes the pain dissolve," I said.

"It's effective. I use hand-holding all the time with my patients," he said.

When my hand was warm, we walked to the room where the cardiologist was waiting for us.

"How did the test go?" he asked. He had been Dr. Keatinge's colleague for years, and he enjoyed contributing to his studies. He was always eager to discuss the team's findings.

"It went well. The cannulas showed that the blood flow in Lynne's hand wasn't regulated at the wrist level; it was regulated at the fingertips," Dr. Keatinge said.

"That is exciting, something I've never heard before," the cardiologist said.

"It's extraordinary. We need to take a closer look at the data, of course, but I think this may change the way we look at blood flow into the hand," Dr. Keatinge said.

The cardiologist assured me that it would be easier to remove the cannulas than it had been to insert them. He carefully removed the tape and slid a long tube from my wrist, applied heavy pressure to the vein with one hand, covered the incision site with gauze, and secured it with tape.

His face was red and he was sweating.

I was relieved one cannula was out.

He steadied himself, pulled the second cannula out of my artery, applied heavier pressure, and bandaged the incision site.

"There, I'm finished," he said.

"Well done," I said with great relief.

An hour or so later Dr. Keatinge and I walked to his car parked a few blocks from the university. I was more exhausted than after the first test. It was difficult to walk at Dr. Keatinge's pace. His strides were long and he was deep in thought. He stopped walking and asked if he could look at my arm.

I pulled my sleeve up. It was purple and blue from my wrist to my elbow. He touched it gently. It was swollen.

"Do you think I should put ice on it?" I said to make him laugh, but he thought it was a good idea. And he asked if my hand was more numb than after the first test.

It was.

He shook his head and said I probably had some nerve damage. It would take two or three months for the nerves to regenerate. He said he would never ask me to repeat that test. But he would ask me to participate in other tests, and I was eager to do so. We were discovering things about my physiology that were surprising.

A year or so later, Dr. Keatinge asked me to return to the University of London. He led the way into the lab, where three researchers were checking monitors. Off to the side of the room was a plastic Jacuzzi the size of a large bathtub.

The Jacuzzi jets were turned on high. The room was filled with the sounds of bubbling, gushing, and gurgling water. The air flowing around the Jacuzzi was damp and chilly.

Dr. Keatinge asked me to sit in the water for as long as I could tolerate it. He said that they knew I could maintain my core temperature when I swam in cold water, but they wanted to see if I could maintain it if I sat in cold water.

He explained that they had to make sure the water circulated around my body. He said that if the water was still, my body would give off heat and warm a thin layer of water around my body. That would keep me warm and help maintain my core temperature. But he wanted to see the effect of the cold on my body, so he needed to make sure the water was moving around me.

I dipped my hand into the Jacuzzi. "Feels like ten degrees centigrade," I said.

Dr. Keatinge looked surprised.

"I've always been able to put my hand in the water and feel the temperature. Doesn't everyone do that?"

"No, most people can't do that," he said.

"It's probably from all my years of swimming. When you spend a lot of time in the ocean your body becomes more aware of changes in water temperature, buoyancy, and salinity. You feel a big difference when the water temperatures changes just one degree," I said.

I was wired up like I had been for the first cold-hand test.

I gathered the leads and handed them to a tall researcher with brown hair and light brown eyes. Dr. Keatinge introduced us, but I didn't hear his name or those of the other two researchers assisting him. I was nervously adjusting my swimsuit straps.

Dr. Keatinge instructed me to climb into the Jacuzzi and sit in the water for as long as I could tolerate it. He said this test would be a lot easier than putting my hand in ice water.

I nodded, took a deep breath, climbed over the Jacuzzi ledge, and sat down. The cold water bubbled around my neck and shoulders and the jets shot icy water onto my skin. I felt the hairs on my arms stand up.

"Is it okay if I move my arms?" I asked.

"It's okay if you move around a bit, but we don't want you to move much. Your muscular activity will create heat, and we want to see your response to the cold when you are sedentary," he said.

That was going to be difficult. Cold water stimulated me to swim fast and create heat to warm my core. I fought my urge to move, and my urge to shiver. Tightening my muscles and jaw, I imagined closing down blood flow to my arms and legs and pushing the blood into my core to keep my brain and vital organs warm. It took a lot of focus and energy to fight the cold.

"Lynne, are you okay?" Dr. Keatinge asked.

"I am," I said.

I had sat in a hot-water Jacuzzi, but not one filled with cold water. My mind anticipated relaxing heat, but my body experienced exhilarating cold. It was so strange. I laughed.

"Okay, I'll need to leave for a while, but I'll be back to check on you and see how the team is doing," he said.

It was a lot easier sitting in cold water than putting my hand in ice water.

A few minutes later I heard a researcher talking. I couldn't tell what he was saying, but he and the two other researchers were standing by a monitor, staring at it, and then glancing at me.

A tall researcher walked over and checked the Jacuzzi jets. He stuck a pool thermometer in the water and waited a few minutes. He walked to his colleagues and showed them the thermometer.

They turned switches off and on, checked their monitors, and discussed something. They didn't seem to be agreeing.

"We're quite baffled. The water temperature was ten degrees centigrade when you first sat in the Jacuzzi, but within two minutes it increased by a bit more than one degree centigrade," he said.

"That's almost two degrees Fahrenheit," I said.

"Yes. At first we thought there was a malfunction with the equipment. But we checked everything and the equipment is working fine. We decided to add cooler water to the Jacuzzi to bring the water temperature down to ten degrees centigrade. But a few minutes after we did that, the water temperature increased again by more than one degree centigrade," he said.

"How's my core temperature?"

"It's increased half a degree centigrade—about one degree Fahrenheit. We don't know how this could happen. When we tested other subjects in the cold Jacuzzi their core temperatures almost immediately dropped. Do you know how you're able to do this?" he asked.

"I concentrate on feeling the warmth generated in the lower left side of my abdomen. But I don't know how that could warm the water in the Jacuzzi."

He looked at me, then looked down and cleared his throat. "Did you . . . ?" He hesitated.

Suddenly I realized what he wanted to ask and said, "No, I didn't pee in your pool."

He looked up and tried to compose himself. He pressed his lips together.

"Gross. You think I would pee in your pool?" I asked, laughing.

He and the other researcher laughed and he said, "We couldn't figure out how you could pee enough to warm the entire Jacuzzi. We calculated it. We realized that you couldn't put out that much volume."

"The things you have to contemplate," I said.

"Sorry, we need to add more cold water to bring the temperature down," he said.

"Okay," I said. This experiment was helping me learn how to think to warm my core. It was the first time I realized I could endure the cold water without moving. I wanted to stay in the Jacuzzi and see how much longer I could tolerate the cold, but Dr. Keatinge said he had what he needed. He was ecstatic.

Years later, I met Loree Kalliainen, a hand surgeon and assistant professor at the University of Minnesota. I mentioned Dr. Keatinge to her and she said she had read about the tests Dr. Keatinge conducted on me. She explained that the studies informed her about blood flow into the hand for surgeries and she said his work was basic medical research. It would be used by many other physicians and researchers. His findings would eventually help physicians understand how to use cold to reduce the effects of spinal cord injuries, to improve treatment following heart attacks, and for heart surgeries.

Dr. Keatinge's tests also helped me realize that my body and mind could do things I never imagined. I would become the first person to swim in only a swimsuit more than a mile in 32 degrees Fahrenheit (0 degrees centigrade) in Antarctic waters and a quarter of a mile in 26.6 degree Fahrenheit (−2 degree centigrade) in the sea off Greenland. Science inspired me to adapt the testing process to myself and pioneer paths across distant oceans.

5

SCIENCE AND MAGIC

It was as if I had been given magical powers, and all I wanted was to test them. I began thinking about attempting swims that had never been accomplished and using swims to explore the world.

I opened my *National Geographic Atlas* and studied the blue spaces between the continents. I was looking to the far north and far south where the seas would be frigid and rough, where ships would have difficulty sailing.

I spotted the Beagle Channel on the map, the waterway between Argentina and Chile, and remembered reading the *Voyage of the* Beagle, Charles Darwin's book about his journey of exploration and the insights that led to his theory of evolution.

I measured the distance across the strait from Argentina to Chile. In a straight line, it was three miles between the two countries. The Beagle Channel is one of the roughest, coldest, and most dangerous waterways in the world. And the timing for the project wasn't the best. Tensions between Argentina and Chile were high. Despite the political challenges, I was able to meet with the Chilean and Argentine ambassadors to the United States and their naval attachés and I convinced them that a swim across the Beagle Channel could be a gesture of goodwill. If I was successful, the result might be the same as when I swam across the Bering Strait to help open the border between the United States and the Soviet Union and promote peace. I explained to the ambassadors that the success of the Beagle Channel swim would depend upon the navigational support and expertise of the Argentine and Chilean navies.

The day the navies selected—January 13, 1990—was perfect. The water mirrored the bright blue heavens and Hector Alvarez, a captain in the Argentine navy, said, "It is the calmest I have ever seen the Beagle Channel. God has blessed the waters for your swim."

Dr. Keatinge, Dr. Penny Neild, his colleague from the University of London, and Barry Binder, my friend from California, climbed onto the Chilean ship. Ross Roseman, another friend from California, got on a paddleboard beside me.

We started from Argentina and I swam between the two naval ships. The water was a cold 42 degrees Fahrenheit (5.5 degrees centigrade) and the currents were strong, but I swam fast and knew I was creating more heat than I was losing. I looked at the faces of the men on the ships. They were tense.

They knew the water was dangerously cold. They never swam in the channel. But as I got into my pace, I could see their expressions change. They were surprised at my speed and they gained confidence in me. They looked at the shore and at me to measure the distance I needed to swim. They grinned when they realized that what I was attempting was possible. I felt their excitement. They were athletes and athleticism was the thing that connected us—the expression of the human heart and spirit, the thing that transcended differing politics and culture.

Ross was paddling beside me and encouraging me. Dr. Keatinge, Dr. Neild, and Barry were watching and smiling. I asked Ross to tell everyone that seeing them beside me and their reflections in the water was one of the most beautiful things I had experienced. We were achieving the crossing together.

The sea remained calm, but the currents grew strong, and I fought them and the cold and swam seven miles to Puerto Williams, Chile, in three hours and ten minutes. It was my longest, coldest swim, but, just as important, three years later the American ambassador to Bolivia would tell me that my Beagle Channel swim set a precedent for cooperation between Argentina and Chile: the presidents of Argentina and Chile met in the middle of the Strait of Magellan and signed a mineral rights treaty.

My swims were far more than athletic achievements.

My goal was to bring people and countries together in new ways and to improve relations between nations.

Each time I completed a challenging swim I learned something, and I wanted to use what I had learned to take on even greater and more complex challenges.

I spend months and even years preparing for each swim. I don't always make progress during my training. Sometimes workouts are tedious, and I get bored, distracted, or tired. Most of the time I love to be in the water, but sometimes I don't feel like working out. Sometimes I need to take time off to rest and recover before getting my mind and body back in the water.

When I swim, I feel a spiritual connection to the oceans, to God, and to the universe. The ocean is the place I can always go when I am seeking solace and when I am happy. No matter where I travel in the world, the water feels like home.

When I am swimming I feel like a musician discovering nuances in sound, color, and rhythm. My body is the instrument and the ocean is the symphony. I immerse myself in music and hear and feel the ocean's movements. We create music together. I hear the driving beat of my arms and legs and the song of my breath and bubbles.

Like a musician, I improvise. My stroke changes with the rise and fall of the seas, with the wind, water density, and current. The music shifts in harmony with the changing surface of the sea, the temperature of the water, the salinity, wind, current, tide, and the melody playing inside my mind. I am a part of the ocean. It is a part of me and we are playing a duet.

In the ocean I feel the energy waves from the sun, moon, wind, and rotation of the planet, and I am surrounded by the energy of life from the tiniest plankton to fish, dolphins, seals, and enormous whales. Sometimes I hear their voices, and the song of the surf, the melody of the moon through her ebbing and flooding tides, and the wind blowing across the water. The ocean is always a musical and magical place.

In the darkness of early morning, my arm strokes jostle millions of plankton. A chemical reaction occurs in their bodies. They turn the black water sparkling phosphorescent blue. I wonder about life, the universe, and my place in it. I feel the warmth in my body, the cold ocean surrounding me, and I watch fish swimming fathoms below me lighting the depths of the ocean like the stars and planets light the depths of the universe. I wonder how the stars can burn so bright without losing their heat to the frigid heavens.

I watch the rosy sun rise from the dark blue ocean and see it change color and create waving rivers of crimson, orange, yellow, and white light. The onshore breeze wakes the world like a gentle morning kiss. When I train I think about my life, my passions, and what is in my heart. I list the things I need to do each day and the things I want to do. But I also dream about what I can do, and that makes life rich and exciting.

I started to think about what else I could do. I was considering a swim that would be more challenging than the Beagle Channel. One that was colder, and higher, and had never been swum. I began to realize that when I attempted a swim, I was taking two journeys—one where I asked myself, Can I do it? and the other, a physical journey. It was the external challenge posed by the elements—the waves that toss you into the air, the currents that tangle you up and push you in every direction but the direction you want to go. And the winds that blow so hard they push you and your support boat far off course. You have to maintain a confident inner course, that you can and will accomplish your journey, and you have to maintain a powerful outer course, that you have the strength, power, and endurance to move through, across, and over the physical elements.

I opened the atlas and decided I wanted to do something different. I studied the continents and saw Lake Titicaca. It is the highest navigable lake in the world. I contacted a friend at the State Department, made official contacts in Bolivia and Peru, and discovered that Lake Titicaca had never been swum.

The lake is in the Andes Mountains in Bolivia and Peru, at 12,500 feet (3,810 meters).

In 1983 I swam across three glacial lakes in New Zealand's Southern Alps. Lake Tekapo is at 2,296 feet (700 meters). I swam 3.7 miles (6 kilometers) across the lake in one hour and twenty-six minutes. The combined effects of cold and altitude made the swim challenging. Lake

Titicaca was more than 10,000 feet higher than Lake Tekapo, but I remembered that Sir Edmund Hillary trained to become the first person to climb Mount Everest by hiking around Lake Tekapo and climbing 12,218 feet (3,724 meters) to Mount Cook's summit.

A friend put me in touch with Dr. Robert "Brownie" Schoene, a pulmonary specialist and researcher who was a member of the 1981 American team that summited Mount Everest. Brownie was intrigued with this challenge and the associated research and suggested that I meet him in Colorado so he could guide me through my acclimatization process. He would observe me to make sure I didn't experience altitude sickness or high-altitude pulmonary edema (HAPE), a life-threatening condition in which fluid accumulates in the lungs.

Brownie met me at the Denver airport. He was lean, medium height, had wavy brown hair, dark brown eyes, and a deep, calm voice. We drove to Montezuma, a town at an altitude of 10,312 feet (3,143 meters). It was a place where he did research and clinical work, rock climbed, and trained to climb mountains. During the drive I asked him why I felt colder during my Mount Cook swims than when I swam at sea level. Brownie's eyes lit up. He was a kindred spirit. He loved exploring the limits of human ability and answering questions. He explained that wind and water moving over the body's surface wick heat away faster than any other method. And air at altitude tended to be drier and therefore able to facilitate heat loss by evaporation. Breathing cold air also caused heat loss.

For two days I walked and rested. During the exercise periods, I breathed harder and my heart beat faster, but I didn't show any signs of altitude sickness—I didn't experience headaches or have difficulty breathing, so Brownie drove us to 8,000 feet (2,438 meters). We hiked along a mountain road for a couple of hours, and I did fine, so we drove to 9,000 feet (2,743 meters) and looked for an alpine lake where I could swim, but they were all frozen. Brownie thought if I could ski, exercising at altitude would help me acclimate, but I was not a good skier. I had a stretch cord—a long resistance band—and if I attached one end to a tree and put my hand in each handhold I could lean over and pull my arms like I was swimming.

We agreed that I'd use my stretch cord to exercise at the top of the mountain. As I rode up the ski lift, I watched the earth drop below. I felt my heart beating faster and realized that this was the start of another great adventure.

A man helped me off the chairlift and looked at me like I was strange. I wasn't wearing skis. He asked me if I was okay. I said I was fine, and that I was training to swim Lake Titicaca. He laughed and said the manager had called him to tell him that I would be there, but he thought the manager was joking. He pointed to a stand of tall dark green pine trees lining the edge of the slope, said I could tie my cord to one of the trees, and wished me luck.

I found a tall, sturdy pine, with thick bark so my cord wouldn't irritate the tree, tied the cord to the trunk, and began swimming. My breathing and heart rate increased.

The air was perfumed with pine and sweet snow. I monitored my breathing and checked my heart rate. I was fine. so I took two steps back into deep snow, put more resistance on the cord, and pulled much harder. The sudden movement released snow from the tree's branches, and it dropped in a pile and covered me from head to toe.

Laughing, I worked into my swimming pace, and when I was warm, took off my coat. I thought I should have worn my swimsuit. The air temperature was around freezing, much colder than the air temperature at Lake Titicaca, and that would help me be better prepared.

Skiers sped by me. Some looked at me like I was crazy, a few stopped to ask what I was doing. When I told them I was training to swim across Lake Titicaca, they laughed, but when they realized I was serious, they asked about my training and wished me luck. They inspired me.

I "swam" for two hours and was exhausted when I finished but couldn't wait to talk with Brownie. He was confident I would be able to acclimate for Lake Titicaca. He told me how to continue training. He said to move slowly when I landed in La Paz, Bolivia, and to sleep. La Paz's altitude was between 10,500 and 13,000 feet (3,200 to 3,962 meters). The next couple of days he suggested that I walk around the city and take it easy.

I flew to La Paz. Barry Binder, Deborah Ford, and Pete Kelly—all friends from California— would join me a week later. Charles Bowers, the American ambassador to Bolivia, put me in touch with the Bolivian minister of defense, who promptly offered to provide a Bolivian naval boat and two of his naval officers to navigate for me. They patrolled the lake and knew the weather patterns and currents. They were happy to help. Ambassador Bowers also introduced me to Paul Fernandes, a colleague. Paul was a British biologist working with the Bolivian government to study and help sustain fish populations in Lake Titicaca.

Paul and his friend gave me a ride to Copacabana, a small town on the lake, and invited me to travel with them by boat to Isla del Sol, Island of the Sun, a desolate island in the southern part of the lake. Isla del Sol was known as the birthplace of the Incas and the Aymara Indians.

On May 19, 1992, I walked into Lake Titicaca. The air temperature was fifty-seven degrees Fahrenheit (fourteen degrees centigrade) and the water temperature was fifty degrees Fahrenheit (ten degrees centigrade), but they both felt much colder.

When I started swimming freestyle I felt great, so I pulled stronger, but I wasn't getting enough oxygen. I was gasping for air but couldn't catch my breath. What do I do now? I asked myself. Roll over onto your back so you can breathe.

Floating on my back, I wondered, How am I ever going to swim ten miles (sixteen kilometers) across the lake if I can't swim one hundred meters? Had I overestimated my ability? What made me think I could do this?

I looked into the sky. The sun at altitude was blazing white, the sky was cerulean blue, and the searing white glare on the calm lake made me squint even though I was wearing tinted goggles. The low-pressure altitude, cold water, and my breathing were causing my body to lose heat quickly and my muscles were tightening to block the chill. I needed to swim fast to create heat to get warm, but I couldn't swim fast and get enough oxygen. What could I do?

Swim slowly. Swim breaststroke. Breathe deeply. I swam breaststroke, caught my breath. I realized that if I was going to attempt the swim I would need to choose between being warm and breathing. Swimming across Lake Titicaca was going to be far more difficult than I imagined.

Would ten days be enough time to acclimate?

For the next week, I swam in the morning along the shores of Copacabana, with its bright yellow, red, blue, pink, and green buildings edging the lake. A small herd of long-horned brown and white steers with big dark brown eyes stood knee-deep in the lake. They turned their heads in sync and watched me as I swam back and forth. I don't think they had ever seen anyone swimming in the lake, and even the local people stopped and stared when they saw me swimming along the shore, but the hotel owner where I was staying told them that I was training to swim across Lake Titicaca to celebrate the peaceful existence of the Bolivians and Peruvians who lived around the lake, and after that, they watched and waved, and said, *"Buena suerte"*—good luck.

At the hotel I couldn't figure out how to use the shower. There were two electrical wires that hung above a metal box. The hotel owner explained that I needed to connect the electrical wires while I was standing in the shower to heat the water. He said it was a good idea to wear rubber sandals. I didn't take many hot showers after that!

On May 26, 1992, my friends from California, a representative from the United States embassy, and a reporter from Peru climbed into the Bolivian navy's boat and the two officers steered to a beach below the city of Copacabana.

I walked into the water and began swimming toward Chimbo, Peru, on the opposite side of the lake. The water was calm and clear, and when I looked down, hundreds of frogs as long as my foot were resting on the sandy bottom. They were pale green and whitish gray. Their mouths were wide open and their arms and legs outstretched. They didn't move when I touched them with my big toe. They looked eerie and gave me an unsettled feeling. I swam next to the boat and tried to get into my pace. I was having difficulty. I was trying to find a balance between my breathing and working hard enough to keep myself warm. When I tried to increase my pace, I couldn't get enough oxygen, and when I slowed down, I felt the cold piercing my skin. Once that happened, I never felt warm again. The cold bored into my muscles. They felt as tight as a board. I focused on making them relax. The water was calm, but large puffy cumulus clouds shaded me from the sun, and the air temperature plummeted. But when a strong breeze pushed the clouds away, the sun's rays were hot on the water's surface. I pulled more under my body to gain more lift so I could feel the sunlight warming my back.

About halfway across the lake, the wind began blowing at ten to fifteen knots, the water erupted into whitecaps, and I swam into the waves. My speed dropped and I wondered if I would reach the other side.

My crew cheered me on and that lifted my spirits. I told myself each stroke brought me closer to the finish.

Three-fourths of the way across the lake, I was cold and exhausted; I hadn't expected the altitude to affect me so much. I had to roll onto my side and inhale to get enough oxygen. Waves were crashing around me; I inhaled spray and choked. I stopped to catch my breath. The wind increased, and the waves broke faster. Because of the rough water, I changed my stroke pattern, used my arm to shield my mouth, and breathed into my armpit.

Lifting my head, I looked toward shore. It looked far away and I wondered if I could reach it. I put my head down, continued swimming, and felt the wind swing around and the waves change direction. I was surfing the lake, being pushed by the current, and swimming at a faster pace than I had ever swum.

"See the people coming down from the hills?" Deborah shouted.

There were women walking toward the beach with their llamas.

"They're coming to welcome you," Barry shouted.

As I reached shore, Deborah jumped into knee-deep water and wrapped a beach towel around me. I was cold but not shivering. I heard people cheering and shouting in Spanish and in English. They were off to our left, wearing bright red sweat suits.

The group of Aymara Indians stood in front of us and stared. And I'm sure I stared back. They wore interesting traditional clothes. The women wore black bowler hats, with their hair in long black braids. Their colorful shawls, sweaters, and woolen skirts were blown by the wind. The men were dressed in thick work clothes and bowler hats.

One man said they had been listening to the radio about the swim. They had never seen anyone swim in the lake and they wanted to see the swimmer. One of the people wearing a red sweat suit told me that he was a member of the Bolivian national swim team. They had walked from Bolivia to Peru to watch the swim. I couldn't believe they had walked all the way around the lake. They were excited. We talked about their training and spoke with the Aymara people about the majesty of the lake and their special part of the world, where people who lived around the lake were friends.

The people in Copacabana celebrated the completion of the swim with flowers and sweets and we posed for photos together.

An international group of runners—the Hash Hound

Harriers, who worked for the embassies in La Paz—
invited me to join them on a run to the 18,000-foot peak
of a nearby mountain. If I couldn't run I could walk, or
just have a hot drink with them at the base of the peak at
a café at 16,000 feet. I knew I couldn't run to 18,000 feet.
I couldn't run at sea level, but I wondered what it would
feel like to walk to the 18,000-foot summit. I was unsure.
I almost died on a swim in the Nile River from being sick
and pushing too far when I should have climbed out of
the water. I wondered if I would be pushing too far. But I
had to go. I wanted to see what I'd never seen and experience as much as I could.

Four Range Rovers climbed steep roads with sheer
drops on either side and no guardrails. The local people
had their vehicles blessed by a priest at the cathedral in
Copacabana to keep them safe during their drives.

When we arrived at the base of the peak, I climbed out
of the Range Rover and took a deep breath. The air felt
much thinner and it was hard to breathe.

The Harriers started running up the mountain, and
I stood in awe and watched them. They were amazing
athletes. One soft-spoken confident man who had sandy
blond hair and light blue eyes and looked rugged stayed
behind and offered to climb with me to the summit. I
looked at the mountain. It was steep and covered with
loose shale. I doubted I could do it, and if I attempted it,
I thought I would break my arm or neck on the descent.
He encouraged me to try, and I knew I had to. I climbed

one hundred meters and said I would much rather watch him run up the mountain.

Within moments, he disappeared into the clouds and returned an hour later, ahead of his friends. They were amazing athletes.

When I returned home, I wondered if the extra hemoglobin my body had produced to acclimate to altitude would help me perform better at sea level. I continued working on more challenging projects. In 2002, I swam in Antarctica from the icebreaker *Orlova* in 32 degree Fahrenheit water (0 degrees centigrade). An experienced support crew and three physicians monitored me during the swim. I reached the shores of Neko Harbor in twenty-five minutes, having swum 1.2 miles (1.9 kilometers). It was my most challenging swim, and it was satisfying to complete. But I wondered what more I could do. In 2007, I built on everything I had learned through all my years of swimming and exploring and swam across Disko Bay, Greenland. I jumped into 26.6 degree Fahrenheit water (−3 degrees centigrade) and swam four hundred meters. It was the most intense swim I ever attempted. The water was liquid ice, so cold I couldn't put my face in for a second.

It was so cold I never caught my breath. I swam faster than ever before in my life. And each second I was in the water I had to convince myself to keep swimming. I swam for five minutes and ten seconds. The water on the north side of Disko Bay warmed up to 28.8 degrees

Fahrenheit (−1.8 degrees centigrade), but I didn't notice any temperature change.

I climbed out onto icy rocks and with help from my crew stood up and walked to a snowy area and put on my sweat suit and running shoes. I had succeeded but realized I had reached my limit. The human mind and body were amazingly strong and powerful, but they are also fragile.

6

NOVEMBER 2012—ALARMS

Sandra Field, a longtime friend, had convinced me to join her and others in Costa Rica for Thanksgiving. It was the first Thanksgiving since my mom's death, and Sandy said I needed to take a break. After university, I had moved back home to help my mom and dad. Their health was starting to fail. Sandy told me that I had been caring for my parents for twenty-five years. I hadn't realized that it had been so long. One year blended into the next. Sandy said that in all those years she had never seen me take a vacation. I needed a break.

She was right—I was worn out—and sad. She thought that being in Costa Rica would be fun. Once there, we went zip-lining, jumping off platforms attached to chicle trees twelve stories high and flying from tree to tree at thirty-five miles an hour. We went white-water rafting and were bounced, turned, spun in the rapids, and thrown into the river, but I didn't feel a rush of adrenaline. I felt flat, exhausted, hot, and my feet were swollen.

Dr. Ed Schlenk, a friend from Iowa who was a pathologist and nuclear medicine specialist, e-mailed me about his upcoming travels, and I wrote back. When he discovered that my feet were swollen, he said that swollen feet could signal a heart condition. He advised me to see a cardiologist.

Back home, the swelling had subsided, and for a couple of weeks I thought I was better, but during the night my feet started swelling again, and my calves and hands cramped. The cramping was intense. I stretched my legs, drank water, ate bananas and oranges to replace electrolytes. That helped, but I was scared. My hands had never cramped before.

I hadn't been feeling well for about a month and I was starting to feel worse. Just before Christmas, the Simonelli family invited me to meet them at Disneyland to celebrate their daughter Liana's thirteenth birthday.

I was very tired, but I didn't want to miss the celebration. The drive to Disneyland only took half an hour, but it took another half hour for me to walk the mile from my car in the parking lot to the restaurant. My heart was beating so fast, I had to stop every two hundred meters and rest until I had enough energy to resume walking.

The Simonellis were waiting for me. We ordered quickly. Liana, the birthday girl, and Pearl, her younger sister, were so excited about going on the rides that they talked and ate fast. Liana asked if I would join them on the rides, and normally I would have loved to, but I imagined what it would feel like to be spun, dropped, and inverted, so I told them I would join them next time. As soon as they finished lunch the family raced to Downtown Disney, and I walked back to the car. Now I had to stop every hundred meters to catch my breath. I thought it was because I was under a lot of stress.

That night I barely slept. I was restless, and my breathing was very fast. Suddenly I couldn't control my hands; they were cramping so hard that my thumbs were touching my little fingers. The pain was so intense it took my breath away. I tried to pry one hand open with the other. I couldn't do it. What was wrong with me? I was so in touch with my body, but I couldn't figure out what was going on.

I tried to think what to do. I knew the cause: it was too much stress. There were so many changes in my life, things I had no control over, and I didn't know how to cope.

The cramps in my hands were becoming more intense. I gritted my teeth and pressed my fingers down on the edge of a counter with all my weight. It stretched my hands, but when I stopped pressing down, they began cramping again.

Maybe I was still dehydrated. I drank two more glasses of water. Maybe my electrolytes were still out of balance. I ate another orange. My calcium levels could be low. Drinking a glass of milk might make some difference.

In an hour, the cramping stopped, but then I noticed that I was breathing fast and my heart was beating rapidly. Must be from the pain and worry, I thought, and placed my index finger on my carotid artery, near my throat. I felt my pulse, looked at my wristwatch, and counted the number of heartbeats in one minute. My normal rate was sixty beats per minute, but I counted more than one hundred.

Normally my heartbeat felt strong and evenly paced, but now it felt weak and irregular. Something was wrong.

Maybe the fluid retention was causing the leg cramps. Maybe it was something worse. Maybe my heart wasn't pumping enough blood to supply oxygen to my muscles. Maybe they were starving for oxygen. Maybe there was something wrong with my heart. My heart was a muscle; what would happen if it didn't get enough oxygen?

I felt my pulse again. My heart was beating faster. I didn't want to see a doctor. I had spent so much of my life seeing doctors with my parents. One or the other had been sick off and on for twenty-five years. My dad had cancer, an aneurism, a seven-bypass heart surgery, and blockages in his intestine that were always emergency situations. Caring for him was stressful for my mom. Her health declined. She fell and broke her hip, then her pelvis, then her wrist, and her heart started wearing out. She had three leaky heart valves. They fought to recover from each setback. They fought for their lives. They did that over and over again, and they never gave up. Their minds and spirits were resilient, but their bodies were wearing out. I held their hands during the countless emergencies and the months of rehab, and tried to help them adjust to the world as their bodies declined. I loved them so much. They took great care of me when I was a child, supported me when I was a teenager, and gave me the confidence to realize that I could do anything I wanted with my life.

They were always there for me and I needed to be there for them. But it was hard living with them, caring for them, watching one decline, then the other. I always felt a mixture of hope that they would recover again and sadness that they might not.

One parent would be weak and coming out of the hospital, the other going in with an emergency. Sometimes I felt like I would break from the stress. I felt so alone. But I had Cody, the Labrador that I adopted from a neighbor. He was one of my best friends.

Cody helped me take care of my parents, sat with my mom and dad when they were ill. He would lean against them and put his big yellow head in their laps. They would pet his head and they would relax. He looked at them with so much love in his eyes. And he took care of me. He picked up my shoes with his mouth to tell me it was time to go for a walk, and if I didn't move, he would retrieve his leash and drop it in my lap. He loved to make me laugh. He would walk with his leash in his mouth through the neighborhood, and if a neighbor had an open door he would walk into their homes, and I would hear them say, "Oh, it's Cody! Come on inside."

They would pet him and give him treats and he would smile and lean against them. He loved people and most dogs. He rarely barked but held his tail high and wagged it as he walked. He made me happy and I loved him.

I didn't want to see a doctor and begin that process of decline. I didn't want to discover that something was wrong with me.

I was sure the stress was getting to me. My dad died, my mom died, and then Cody died. I felt so sad and alone.

With time my sadness and loneliness grew worse, not better. But my heart hurt and the pain intensified. It filled my entire being.

I wanted to sit and do nothing, but I decided that I needed to get out of the house, change my focus. Working out would help me focus on my body, reduce my stress, and make me feel better. I did a two-hour workout in the gym. I tried to work out hard, but I felt too tired.

When I returned home I didn't feel any better. I sat on the couch. My breathing sounded strange, like I was wheezy, but I didn't have allergies. I sounded like my mom a year before she died.

But I still thought I was just feeling a lot of stress. A couple of months earlier, I had seen a doctor, and she did a physical so I could change health insurance companies. She ran the usual tests, and everything came back fine.

But now something had changed. I missed my mom. My best friend. Everything in the house reminded me of her—her paintings, murals, and needlepoints. And there were holes in the house where her things had been removed. The chair where she sat to read was empty.

There was a hole in my world that would never be filled. It was life, but it was hard. I was lucky I had good friends. They understood what I was going through.

When my friend Laura King lost her mom she was so sad she couldn't speak for almost a week. It was hard to comprehend the depths of her feelings until I experienced them myself.

We had been friends for almost thirty years. We met when she wanted me to teach her children and her mom to swim. They became great swimmers and our families became close friends.

She was a doctor, a dermatologist, and I decided to call her. She would know what to do. She was in the car with Charlie Nagurka, her fiancé. They were driving somewhere in Los Angeles. Charlie was also a doctor, an internist, and one of the warmest, most jovial, and positive people I had ever known.

I told Laura I wasn't feeling well.

She said that was strange; I always felt well. She was concerned.

I explained that my heart was beating fast and I mentioned that I had been in touch with Ed Schlenk, a retired radiologist who worked in Iowa and at Scripps in San Diego. He had recommended that I see a cardiologist, but I had waited to see if my symptoms would improve.

Laura asked me to take my heart rate.

It was more than one hundred beats per minute

She asked me how long it had been beating that fast.

For a couple of days, I said.

"A couple days?" she asked with disbelief.

"Yes."

"That's a long time," she said. Her voice was tense.

Charlie asked me what my normal heart rate was.

Sixty beats per minute.

He said I needed to see a cardiologist immediately. Laura agreed. She would call a friend to see if he could fit me in.

I thanked her but said I wasn't sure if I wanted to see a doctor. It made me nervous.

She said she felt the same when she had to see a doctor.

Charlie tried to put me at ease. He said that there were many things that could cause a rapid heartbeat and it might just be stress. It would be good for me to get checked. If my heart started beating faster or if I felt worse, I needed to go to the emergency room, and if I didn't feel as if I could drive, I needed to call 911.

I said if I could see someone Laura knew I would be okay. The last thing I wanted to do was to call the paramedics and go to the emergency room.

Laura said she would call back as soon as she heard from the doctor.

After we hung up, I decided to e-mail Ed Schlenk and let him know I was following up on his advice.

He replied and said it should be checked but was probably a false alarm.

I prayed it was a false alarm. I couldn't deal with being sick.

Laura reached the cardiologist's office. There were three cardiologists she knew in the group. Her physician friends saw them for their heart problems. Dr. Milan Rawal was the youngest in the group. He was available at 3:00 p.m. Laura asked if I could wait that long.

I said I would be fine, but I glanced at my watch. It was 10:00 a.m. Strange, once I accepted that I needed to go to the doctor, I wanted to get in right away and see what was wrong. I wondered if my heart could hold out.

I told myself that I could get back to work. I was supposed to be writing my new book, but I couldn't concentrate. I was supposed to have dinner with Cindy Palin, a good friend. She was going to make her grandmother's Italian chicken recipe. I hoped I would be back from the doctor's office in time. I was also supposed to meet another friend in the morning for a workout at the gym, but I wasn't sure if I would make it.

My goal was to get through this problem as soon as possible. I decided not to eat or drink anything in case I needed to have a test that required sedation. A procedure would have to be delayed if there was anything in my stomach.

I watered the plants in case I had to stay in the hospital for a day or two. Everything was ready for my siblings and their families' arrival. In four days we were to scatter my mom's ashes and Cody's. The house was clean, food was in the fridge, whatever was needed was there.

My heart felt as if it was beating faster. I held my index finger on my carotid artery. It was beating a lot faster. Reading e-mails might distract me.

There was one from Joe, my firefighter friend in Florida. His timing was perfect. He said it was time for me to take care of myself and I needed to take time to grieve. He comforted me by writing that my mom and Cody lived and shared their lives with me so that I would be happy.

"The truth is that they never left you. They have just been transformed. They will be with you, a part of you, forever. And the ashes dispersals are a birthday party not a funeral."

I had told him that I was spending Christmas with the Simonelli family. He wrote that I couldn't wait until Christmas to decompress. I needed to start as soon as I finished reading the e-mail. And I needed to eat my favorite ice cream anytime I wanted. He told me to watch funny movies, fantasize about someone tickling me, get a massage or tell a dirty joke, and call him anytime I wanted to talk. We had been in touch by e-mail, but e-mail was limited.

I imagined calling him as soon as I finished reading his message. He was strong, compact, and lean. He was a mountain climber. I was intrigued that a mountain climber could live in the flatlands of Florida and train to climb mountains. The mountain climbers I knew lived in Washington State, Montana, New Hampshire, and Colorado. They lived where they could climb and acclimate to altitude, and cold.

Joe lives in Florida because of his job, but he was not limited by his environment. He figured out a way to simulate training at altitude. He ran sprints outdoors and simulated breathlessness, and ran long distances to build endurance. In the gym, he wore heavy boots on the Stair-Master. Most people didn't understand. They stared at him, laughed at him, and made fun of him, but he knew it was what he needed to climb mountains.

He thought differently and saw possibilities when other people only saw impossibilities. He impressed me. He was methodical and thoughtful, and he had a lot of heart.

I considered calling him, but I wasn't feeling well and I didn't want to whine on the phone.

Joe e-mailed a second time that morning and asked how I was doing.

I wrote that I had an appointment with a cardiologist in the afternoon.

"Call me. Let's just talk." He e-mailed his phone number to make sure I had it.

It seemed like he was on high alert.

I needed to let him know I was okay. I called him and told him so.

He laughed. He had a warm laugh that put me at ease.

He asked questions: "Are you still living in the same house as you did years ago? Where are you in the house right now? What are you doing? Are you sitting up or lying down?"

His questions seemed strange, so I asked, "Are you asking me this in case you think I need the paramedics?"

"Yes, if the line goes dead, I know where to send them. It's about being prepared," he said.

Wow, I thought, he's smart. It was surreal.

It had been my job to evaluate my parents and figure out if they needed help. Now someone else was doing that for me. I didn't like being evaluated, but I told myself, He's a professional, and he's using everything he knows to help me. Be grateful for that.

Joe was asking if I had been following the news. We discussed world affairs and politics. His views were similar to mine, but his arguments were stronger.

I checked my watch. We had been talking for an hour. I told him that I appreciated his time, but I was sure he had things to do.

He said, "I have nothing more important to do than to talk with you today."

"Joe, I'm just exhausted."

"Have you been feeling this way for a while?"

"I don't want to be sick. I don't want the doctor to find out there's something wrong with me."

"You're going to be okay. Your energy levels are low. When did you last eat or drink anything?"

"Last night," I said.

"You need to eat something. Your blood sugar is low. The food will give you fuel, and that will make you feel better."

I told him I would eat after we hung up.

He insisted that I eat right away.

I felt like a child being told what to do but realized that I wasn't thinking clearly and that he was trying to help me feel better.

There were a couple of tangerines in the refrigerator. The tangerines were sweet, cold, and tasted good. They reminded me of the orange trees my dad planted in the backyard. He loved those trees. He grew up in rural Maine, and on Christmas Day he always found a Florida orange in his Christmas stocking. The orange was the highlight of his Christmas.

It was almost Christmas. I always missed him more at Christmas. Why did all of this have to hurt so much?

I walked into the kitchen to fill a glass with water.

"Are you okay?" Joe asked. His voice was on edge.

"I just got up to get a glass of water," I said.

"You sound breathless," he said.

"I do? I don't feel breathless." Was he being that attentive? What else was he hearing?

"How's your heart rate?" he asked.

"It's slower. Talking with you helped bring it down. Thanks for being here, Joe." I almost started crying and told myself to pull it together. "I'm feeling better now; maybe I don't need to see the doctor."

"You need to," he insisted and then he gave me a pep talk.

It was strange to hear him recount my history, but he

knew everything I had written about. He reminded me of my channel swims, how the tides and currents sometimes pushed me backward, and how I had fought them and succeeded. He told me stories about my swim across the Strait of Magellan and the Bering Strait, how I did things that people thought were impossible. He said I inspired him and that I needed to remember who I was and what I had achieved.

He psyched me up.

"What time do you need to leave for your appointment?" We had been talking for more than three hours.

"In about fifteen minutes."

He told me to pack a bag with a set of clothes, a book, a pen and writing pad, and earplugs. The earplugs would help if I had to spend the night in the hospital and share a room with someone. He asked me to let him know what the doctor said and to call anytime.

"Thank you, Joe, for holding my hand," I said.

"Happy I could help. Look forward to hearing what the doctor says," he said, and his voice sounded bright.

Just as I was leaving home, Laura King called. She said she would meet me at the cardiologist's office, if that was okay. I was grateful and relieved. She would be able to translate anything the doctor told me that I didn't understand and she would be able to ask questions; I wouldn't know what to ask.

7

DECEMBER 18 — DOCTOR'S OFFICE

Taking a deep breath, I opened the door to the cardiologist's office and let the breath out slowly. It was what I did the moment before I jumped from the side of a boat into the ocean. One last breath to carry me through the transition to the shocking cold.

The room was filled with elderly men and women. Some were sitting in chairs and others in wheelchairs. They looked tired, resigned, and frightened. I wanted to step backward and let the door close, turn and walk away. There were a couple of people on oxygen. It was so sad. I wanted to bolt out of there. I had been in too many doctors' offices with my parents. I lived with them and cared for them. They had been on the edge of life for so many years. My dad got bladder and prostate cancer from smoking, and he had to have those organs surgically removed.

During the surgery, the doctors noticed that he had an aneurism on his descending aorta that could have ruptured at any time. They wrapped the aneurism with Teflon, and that prevented it from bursting. The doctors saved his life that day, and they would thirty or forty more times. He was the strongest, gentlest, brightest man I knew. He was a Navy Corpsman in World War II and saved many lives but lost all of his friends. He was someone I could always depend on, but the chemo that saved his life started to break him down, and the scars from his bladder surgery created blockages in his intestine. They were life threatening, and I never knew when they would flare up. My mom was with him most of the time, but she needed help. It was hard being on alert all the time, wondering when the next emergency would happen. And each time we were in the emergency room I prayed, hoped, and wished my dad would live, and somehow he always rallied. His will to live was amazing.

I went to some doctor visits with him and my mom and listened to the news. He needed open-heart surgery. He needed it immediately. We were afraid he would die; he had been through so much. He looked so small and pale on the gurney, but when they brought him to the recovery room he had color in his face. His recovery was a painful six months. He worked so hard. We did too.

But my dad's health continued to decline. My world became small and compressed, and I wondered how much longer I could be there for them. One time when my dad had to go to the emergency room for another blockage I didn't want to go. I didn't want to watch my dad struggle, to see him in pain, to see him squirm, to hear the other people in the emergency room moaning and crying and fighting for life. I wanted to run away, but no one else was there to care for them. My siblings lived far away. I needed to be strong for him and for my mom. She always had a positive attitude and was cheerful. She looked at me with her dark brown eyes and said my dad was the one who was sick. He was suffering. But I felt like I was too. It was so hard to see him struggling all the time.

My mom never cried in front of me, but she started to break down physically. I think it was from the stress of caring for my dad. Her heart started beating erratically. My dad and I were afraid the doctors wouldn't get it under control and she would die. The doctors put her on medications that helped for a while, but sometimes her heart started beating fast again and it became an emergency.

I didn't sleep well. I was always listening for the next emergency. I wondered what my dad would do if he lost my mom. And I wondered what she would do if she lost him. I could see how much they loved each other and I knew it was the love they had for each other that kept them alive. But it was hard for me. I realized I couldn't have a life. I adopted Cody, a six-year-old yellow Labrador retriever, who became one of my best friends and also helped my parents. My dad was always in pain and was often worried about a blockage. Cody helped him relax.

He would put his big yellow head in our laps and look

at us with his golden brown eyes and wag his tail. He helped me deal with the stress. Still, when one parent was just getting out of the hospital and the other was going in, and I was trying to take care of them both, I would wonder if I would go crazy.

One day my mom and dad were walking Cody and my mom tripped over him and broke her hip. She said he suddenly stepped in front of her. She never blamed Cody for her fall, but she had to have a plate and pin put in her femur to hold it together. And the day after surgery, she was transferred to an assisted care residence, and when she moved she worried we didn't know where she was. When we walked into her room her heart was beating at 198 beats per minute.

The nurse thought she was going to have a heart attack. My dad caressed her soft gray hair and calmed her down and promised that neither he nor I would ever leave her. He tried to keep his promise.

When my dad died, I felt pain I had never experienced in my life. It seemed to pierce my soul. My mom seemed okay until she was given his ashes. Then she broke down. It was heartbreaking to see her like that. And it was heartbreaking not to hear my father's voice, touch his hand, see his face, or give him a hug. I missed him. I asked my mom why she wasn't sad all the time. She said she missed my dad very much, but she had a choice: she could be sad all the time or she could live her life. She remodeled the house, went through a new phase of painting bright abstracts. She went out with me and my friends and they became her friends.

When Cody got sick and I had to have him put to sleep, I couldn't stop crying. My mom told me that Cody had had a good life. It was important to remember the joy and happiness he gave us. She was right. But I missed him so much. It was strange not to wake up with him and take him for a walk. It was strange not to have him near me.

My mom's health declined. She slipped in the lobby at the movies and broke her pelvis and shoulder. When she could walk I took her shopping. She loved to shop and to see new things. We went to the large food and clothing stores, and I gave her a shopping cart for support so she could walk on her own and get strong. Then she tripped and broke her wrist at home. I was upstairs and heard her fall downstairs. I was right there, but I wasn't close enough to help her. The bone in her wrist was poking out and it was bloody and deformed. She said it didn't hurt that much, and at least it wasn't her right arm. She could still paint pictures. I felt so bad for her. I couldn't keep her from getting old, keep her body from falling apart. I was so sad, but I couldn't let her see my sadness. It wouldn't help her.

She fought to regain her health and her life. And I fought each battle with her. But her heart valves started to fail. We went to see the cardiologist often and to the emergency room when her heart started racing. The medications she was taking couldn't control her heart any-more. She was wheezing all the time, and I wondered if that was congestive heart failure, if her lungs were filling with fluid and if she was drowning.

At night I rubbed her back and talked to her softly so she could relax and sleep. She was eighty-four years old, too elderly and weak for surgery. I don't know how many doctor visits we went to. I held her hand tightly, always wanting her to know that I was there for her and I loved her and believed she would get better. She was like Dad. She never wanted to die. She never gave up, but her body gave out. She was my best friend. It was so hard to never again hear her voice, see her smile, hold her hand, or hug her. It was so strange that she was gone. The pain of los-ing her stabbed my soul, and I felt like everything in my life was dying.

And now there was something wrong with me. I didn't want to begin this decline. I didn't want to start falling apart piece by piece.

Couldn't I pretend that nothing was wrong? Life was so tough. I didn't want to see the doctor. I wanted to turn around and run. The people in the waiting room were my parents' age. I didn't want to enter that world. It was terrifying, and painful.

I took another deep breath and walked to the recep-tion area. I was trying to calm my heart, but it was beat-ing fast.

A woman at the front desk asked me my name, told

me to sign in, and handed me a medical history form. It didn't take long to fill it out; I didn't have any preexisting health conditions and I didn't take any medications. The reason I was seeing the doctor was because my heart was beating fast. I wanted to bolt.

A woman in her mid-twenties opened the door to the back rooms and called my name. My heart beat faster. I wished that this was a bad dream.

She opened the door to the exam room: white walls, floor, and ceiling. There was a poster on the wall about varicose veins and an exam table covered with a white paper sheet.

She asked me to roll up my sleeve so she could take my blood pressure. It wasn't elevated. That surprised me. I thought it might be high.

She asked me to take off my shirt and bra and put on a gown that opened in the front.

She applied the twelve EKG patches to my chest and attached the EKG leads.

I watched the machine record my heartbeats.

Dr. Rawal would read the results and discuss them with me. I returned to the waiting area.

It was good to get out of there. I went out to the hall to wait for Laura and paced from one end to the other. I had to walk slowly. My heart was beating fast and I didn't want it to beat faster.

Laura texted me. She was stuck in heavy traffic and would arrive soon.

The office door opened, and a young-looking man with short jet-black hair and dark brown eyes stepped into the hall. He was wearing a white coat. He looked like an athlete. He looked fit, and he had that glow.

"Are you Lynne?" he asked.

"Yes," I said, embarrassed that he had to come out and get me.

"Hi, I'm Milan Rawal."

He reached out his hand and I shook it.

"I need to talk with you about the EKG; can you come back with me to the exam room?" he asked.

"You can't just tell me what's going on out here?" I asked.

He shook his head. "We need to go back to the room. I need to listen to your heart."

I hesitated.

"Is Dr. King here yet?" he asked.

"She's on the way. She's caught in traffic." I thought I would embarrass her if I bolted. I couldn't do that.

I followed Dr. Rawal. He asked me to sit on the exam table.

"What did you do before you came here today?" Dr. Rawal asked.

"I worked out for a couple hours at the gym. Did the elliptical machine on level sixteen for an hour and then an hour spin class and some weights."

He looked surprised.

"You aren't manifesting as expected," he said.

I guess I didn't look that bad. I wasn't surprised. Elite athletes learn to push their bodies as far as they can, and then they push them further. They find a way to eke out whatever strengtrh remains to reach their goal. Athletes mask their pain and fatigue so they don't look weak or vulnerable to a competitor. I was doing that now. I knew my body was working hard, but I didn't want to be sick.

"Have you been short of breath?" Dr. Rawal asked.

"No, I haven't."

"You tolerated the workout without stopping? Maybe you didn't feel as good as you usually do when exercising? Didn't have the same energy?" he asked.

His questions made realize that I was manifesting. That something was wrong with me.

"I didn't stop working out, but I had to do it less intensely. I don't think I realized I was short of breath. I've been stressed, and I thought my breaths were short because of that," I admitted.

He put his stethoscope on my chest and asked me to take a deep breath and hold it. He held his breath and listened, told me to take another breath and hold it. He moved the stethoscope to three different areas above my heart and listened.

Could he hear my heart's song? Could he hear that my heart suffered? Could he hear that it was tired, stressed, and filled with anguish?

He asked me to take a deep breath so he could listen to

my lungs. He was checking to hear if they were clear or if they were filled with fluid. He was intense and focused.

I wondered if every heart he heard was different, if each had its own song.

He studied me. He couldn't imagine how I had worked out as hard as I had that morning with the condition my heart was in.

"Your heart rate is one hundred fifty-seven beats per minute," he said with concern.

One hundred fifty-seven beats per minute, I thought. Wow, that's extremely high. When I'm in the gym and working out faster than my normal pace, it's difficult for me to get my heart rate above 140. That explains why I felt so tired when I was meeting the Simonelli family at Disneyland and had difficulty walking from and to the parking lot.

My heart is close to maxing out when I'm sitting, and it was working harder when I walked. No wonder I had to cut back on my workout at the gym this week. No wonder that when I lifted weights I felt funny and had to stop.

Dr. Rawal was staring at me. "How long has your heart been beating fast?" he asked.

"It has been beating faster than normal for a month, but it started beating a lot faster two or three days ago."

He shook his head.

Not a good sign. He must have seen something in the EKG and heard something in my heart and lungs.

Fortunately he didn't blast me with information and overwhelm me as other doctors did to my parents.

He took the time to explain what was happening. He waited to make sure I could hear and understand it. It was a lot. I couldn't have understood or absorbed it if he didn't tell me in small bits.

Dr. Rawal explained, "Your heart is in atrial fibrillation. AFib is an abnormal heart rhythm. The heart is a pump controlled by an electrical conduction system similar to this room, where there is a switch on the wall and every time it flips it turns on the lights. There is a control chamber in your heart that houses a similar switch, and every time it flips the heart receives a signal. In atrial fibrillation, that control chamber suddenly develops multiple switches, which are all flipping in a barrage of rapid and irregular signals the rest of the heart is trying to keep up with, resulting in the rapid and irregular pulse."

I could comprehend what he was saying. My mom and dad had AFib.

He looked at me and waited to make sure I understood.

I nodded.

Dr. Rawal said, "Patients with AFib can experience many symptoms, including palpitations, shortness of breath, chest pain, exertional fatigue, and dizziness. The long-term consequences of atrial fibrillation can include an increased risk of stroke that would require chronic anticoagulation medication in most patients. Reestablishing normal sinus rhythm—normal heart rhythm—is a strategy that could relieve symptoms by allowing the heart to work in a coordinated manner again."

Oh great, he has to convert my heart, and I'm going to have to go on blood thinners, and go into the laboratory every week or two to have my blood levels checked to make sure my blood isn't too thin. That's what my mom and dad had to do. I don't want to do this. I just want to go home.

Oh God, I wish Laura was here. I wish Charlie was here. I wish Joe was here. But it will be better if I just deal with this, then they won't worry.

"AFib begets AFib—the longer you are in it, the harder it is to get you out. I'd really like to try and convert you as soon as possible. We need to get you into the hospital today to get your heart rate under control."

He had a plan and he was confident. That was good. "How do you do this?" I asked.

"First we need to make sure your heart is safe for cardioversion; by this I mean making sure there aren't any clots present in the heart prior to shocking it. We will do this with a transesophageal echocardiogram (TEE). The control chamber of your heart happens to lie adjacent to your esophagus, and this is where we are most likely to find clots if there are any. I'm going to take an ultrasound probe, about the diameter of my finger, and pass it down your esophagus so that I can get a good look. Of course, you will be well sedated. As soon as I confirm the absence of any clots we will shock your heart with hopes of putting it back into the normal rhythm. We'll reset your heart," he said.

It was amazing that he could reset the human heart.

"Do you do a lot of these conversions?"

"Yes, I do," he said, sounding confident.

"Okay," I said.

"We will try you on rate-control medications first, and if they don't work we will try the cardioversion tomorrow morning."

"Okay," I said.

"All right, then, let's make it happen. I'm going to put in a call and get you a bed," he said.

The hospital was across the parking lot from his office. I thought I could walk that far.

He asked what medications I was taking, if I was allergic to any medications, and if I had had any surgeries.

This information was on the health history form I had filled out before I saw him, but I realized he was confirming what he had read. He was thorough. That was good.

The only time I had been in the hospital was when I was five years old—when I had my tonsils and adenoids taken out.

"You haven't been hospitalized for anything?" he asked, astonished.

"I've been lucky. I've been healthy," I said.

He asked me if I was okay waiting for Laura in the

hallway and said that she could come and see him if she had any questions. He needed to make the calls to see if he could find a room for me.

I walked into the hall and held back tears. This wasn't the way I was supposed to spend the next part of my life. I was supposed to be able to have my own life now. I was supposed to be able to do what I wanted to do. I decided to e-mail Ed Schlenk, the doctor in Iowa. He would have some suggestions.

I wrote to him and said my heart was in AFib. Dr. Rawal was going to try to control the AFib with medications and to start me on blood thinners. If the medications didn't work he was going to shock my heart and start amiodarone to keep me in the normal rhythm.

Ed sent me an e-mail.

He wrote:

You are your own best medical advocate. Always read (wiki and/or e medicine) about your diagnoses and medications. The more you know, the better your decisions. Don't be afraid to take notes and/or bring a friend to your medical appointments.

Atrial fibrillation has several related conditions that you might read about and want to rule out. Hyperthyroidism is an associated condition, but there are many others. The anticoagulants (heparin short term, Coumadin/warfarin long term) are to prevent clots from forming in the atrium since it is contracting erratically. They can travel downstream and do damage.

Your foot swelling is probably due to low cardiac output from the inefficient contractions. The med you mentioned, amiodarone—look it up for side effects so you know what to monitor.

Keep yourself medically informed, and keep me posted. Glad it is (and you are) getting taken care of. We have to be our own "Mom" now. Cheers, Ed.

I remembered that the side effects of long-term usage of amiodarone were peripheral nerve damage, lung damage, and blindness. My mom was on amiodarone when all the other medications no longer worked. She couldn't feel her feet, and she was losing her vision. She kept telling her internist her symptoms, but the internist never told her that it might be caused by the amiodarone. It was because this was her last option.

I was frightened. I didn't think I was that sick.

Just then Laura arrived. She hugged me, asked me how I was doing, and if I had seen Dr. Rawal.

I summarized what had happened and said I was sure I missed some details. She disappeared into his office. I leaned against the wall in the hall.

"Are you okay?" she said when she opened the door.

"I'm okay, but I don't want to be here," I said.

"I know," she said, and she explained that while Dr. Rawal was trying to find a room for me, she would walk with me to the hospital and to admitting. By the time I finished filling out the papers, they might have a room; the sooner I got in and took the meds, the sooner I could leave.

We walked across the parking lot, and she asked me how I was doing.

Much better because she was here.

She led the way to the admitting area of the hospital. She used to work there, and the woman in admitting recognized her. Laura introduced me and explained why I was there.

The woman handed me an admitting form and I read through the pages and signed the release. I had done this so many times for my parents. I never thought I would have to do it for myself.

Two physicians recognized Laura and walked over to say hello, as did a radiologist's wife. It seemed as if she knew everyone in the hospital, and everyone she knew liked her.

Dr. Rawal entered the lobby and walked over to us.

The hospital had a shared room ready and he didn't want to wait for a private room. He wanted to get me going on the medications.

Laura led the way into the room and told me to sit down and get comfortable.

I told her I'd rather stand.

"I don't like to be a patient either," she confessed, smiling.

The nurse arrived in the room and introduced herself.

Laura needed to go and said, "You're going to be fine."

The nurse asked if I had ever had an IV.

I hadn't.

She explained the procedure and asked if I wanted to put on a hospital gown.

"I have the option to wear my own clothes?" I asked.

She nodded.

"That's great," I said.

I could get up and walk the hallway without having to try to hold the gown closed. I could keep my muscles moving and keep them strong.

The nurse started the IV, made sure I knew where to find the call button, and showed me the television remote.

I realized I needed to contact Cindy Palin to let her know I couldn't make dinner, and I needed to tell my friend I wouldn't be at our workout the next morning.

Cindy was heading home from work and said she would stop by on the way.

The nurse came back and said that Dr. Rawal wanted me to move to a private room where it would be quieter and I would be able to get some rest.

The nurse guided me through the hallway. It felt good to get up and move. And for a moment I fantasized about pulling the IV out of my hand and running into the elevator and out of the hospital.

I settled into the new bed. It was a lot quieter. Cindy walked into the room. She had had difficulty finding me. She looked distressed.

I remembered going to my parents' hospital rooms and seeing an empty bed, and suddenly feeling panicked, wondering if they had been moved or if they had died.

"I'm glad you found me. I'm glad you're here," I said.

Cindy's dark brown eyes were opened wide. She was shocked to see me in a hospital bed. She glanced down to regain her composure, sat in a chair across from me, and smiled.

She had been in court and was wearing a dark blue jacket and skirt and a pearl-colored silk blouse. She was an attorney and defended doctors and hospitals.

She hugged me and started talking fast. She said after she read my text message she called her assistant and asked her to run a check on my doctor to make sure I was in good hands. She said Dr. Rawal's record was pristine. He was thirty-eight years old, so he wasn't just out of med school; he was experienced. She spoke with him when she saw him at the nurses' station and was impressed.

"Cindy, only you would run a background check on my doctor."

A few minutes later Dr. Rawal walked into the room. He stood close to the bed, glanced at my feet, and smiled.

I was wearing my bright green Christmas socks with leaping reindeer. Everyone who walked into the room saw them and smiled. Dr. Rawal pulled one sock down and looked at my foot and leg. He pressed his finger into my shin. It left a dimple, but the dimple disappeared faster than it had in the office.

"Looks like the fluid is starting to move out," he said.

He didn't anticipate that I would have any problems during the night, but if I did, he instructed the nurses to call him. If I didn't feel right, I needed to ask them to call him.

The last thing I wanted to do was to wake him up in the middle of the night, especially if he needed to do a procedure on me in the morning.

He must have read my mind. He said he needed me to let him know if I was feeling worse.

I assured him that I would.

He reached out and held my shoulder for a moment and said, "Good."

After he left the room, Martha Kaplan, my book agent and friend, phoned me. She tried to sound calm, but her voice was stressed.

I reassured her that I would be okay and that I could go on the book tour scheduled for August, but said I was worried about getting back in touch with the people who were helping me coordinate the tour.

Martha told me not to worry about the tour now. I just needed to concentrate on getting well.

She asked if it was okay if she updated my editor, Vicky Wilson, and others at Knopf, my publisher. I didn't want them to worry, but Martha said they would want to know, so I said it was okay. I didn't want a lot of people knowing what was happening with me. I was trying to deal with it myself.

I remembered that I hadn't called Emmy, my workout buddy. I felt bad that I hadn't gotten in touch with her sooner. I called her. There was just too much happening. I was having a hard time thinking straight.

Emmy said she would come to the hospital as soon as possible. It wasn't an emergency; I told her to take her time.

She told her husband that I was in congestive heart failure. She thought I was going to die.

When she arrived, Emmy's long brown hair was tousled, her blue eyes were wide open like Cindy's, and she was out of breath.

"I'm glad you called me," she said. She sat beside my bed. She was all wound up.

"I knew something was wrong with you this morning. I called you and when I couldn't reach you, I texted you, and when you didn't respond, I called every emergency room in the area, but this is a little out of the area. I never would have thought of calling here," she said.

She calmed down and settled into the chair.

"I'm glad I came to see you. You look a lot better than I thought you would," she said.

"I'm already getting better. You need a workout partner, and if I'm not there, you won't get to the gym on your own," I teased.

She grinned and wiped tears from her eyes. She told me about what was happening with her family, and I realized that she was trying to give me a sense of normalcy at a time when things were not normal.

She stayed until 9:00 p.m.

I wanted to call Joe, but it was past midnight on the East Coast. I wished it wasn't so late. He said I could call anytime. I wanted to tell him what was happening, but I felt it was too late.

As I lay back in the bed, I realized that each of my friends had given me gifts that day—the gifts of their time, knowledge, positive energy, and love. I was so lucky to have such good friends.

It was almost ten.

Laura called. She had spoken with Dr. Rawal. He said I was responding well to the medications. She wished me good night.

The heart monitor was beeping and displaying the number of times my heart was beating.

My heart rate was fluctuating between 98 and 122 beats per minute. It needed to be lower. I wondered if I could lower it. I wondered if I could do yoga breaths. Breathe in deeply, hold my breath for ten seconds and exhale slowly. I repeated this process three times. That slowed my heart and mind and allowed my body to relax.

I decided to use the heart monitor as a biofeedback tool.

I did the yoga breaths and my heart rate dropped three to five beats per minute. That wasn't good enough.

I needed to escape. I closed my eyes and imagined that I was in the swimming pool, hanging on to the wall. I took a deep breath and pushed off, and I exhaled slowly as I glided through the water. I took three strokes, turned my head and inhaled. I continued swimming until I reached the wall. Took a deep breath and opened my eyes to look at the heart monitor like I would look at the pace clock. My heart rate had dropped by three beats. I pushed off the wall and swam four laps of the pool and checked the heart monitor. My heart was beating three or four beats slower. That wasn't enough. I needed to keep swimming. I kept trying, but I couldn't get it below ninety-five for any significant amount of time.

I closed my eyes and thought about my life—what I had done and what I wanted to do. I thought about the things I had planned and the things I hoped to do. I thought about the people I loved and how much I wanted to spend more time with them. I wondered if I would get well or if it was my fate to decline and die. I wondered if the medications were working.

8

DECEMBER 19—HOSPITAL

It was about 8:00 a.m. when Dr. Rawal walked into the room. He asked me how I was feeling. I was feeling better. My heart was beating slower and I was breathing easier. He said the Lasix was working. It was helping to remove the extra fluid out of my body. My feet and legs were less swollen. The medications they gave me had slowed my heart, but not enough. It was still in AFib and it needed to be converted. He wanted to do the cardioversion as soon as he could get the room and staff.

"If you are able to convert my heart, what is the next step, and if you aren't able to convert it, what will we do?" I asked.

"If we are able to convert your heart to sinus rhythm, the next step will be to optimize medical therapy— giving you medications. If your heart responds and your ejection fraction, or EF, improves, your problem was likely due to tachycardia-induced cardiomyopathy, a persistently elevated heart rate. The condition can ultimately produce significant cardiac structural changes that can result in heart failure (inefficient or insufficient pumping). If not, then we will need to consider a pacemaker and a defibrillator and placement on the heart transplant list," he said.

Cindy Palin walked into the room. She looked like she had been crying. Her eyes and cheeks were bright red, but she smiled and asked me what was happening.

I told her I was better and explained what Dr. Rawal had told me. I was worried about the possibility of having a pacemaker and defibrillator. I didn't want to walk around with appliances in my heart. I wanted to be normal.

"Lynne, I have to tell you, as your good friend, you've never been normal," she said.

She made me laugh hard.

"Take a deep breath. Slow down. You're getting ahead of yourself. Take one step at a time, don't get ahead of yourself," she coached. She was so reasonable.

I took a deep breath, but I hadn't told her the worst part.

"If the defibrillator and pacemaker don't work, Dr. Rawal wants to put me on the heart transplant list at UCLA," I said, and my voice became high-pitched. I didn't want to tell her like that, but I was emotional.

An indecipherable expression crossed her face. I think it was horror, fear, and shock mixed together.

She looked down for a moment, put on her confident face, and repeated, "You are getting ahead of yourself. Take one step at a time."

In my mind, I repeated "one step at a time" over and over. Take this one step at a time. This would be my mantra whenever I was overwhelmed. I knew I was sick, but I never thought I might die.

"Look at what's already happened. You are responding to the meds. Your feet and legs are less swollen. You're breathing easier. Your heart rate is a little slower. You're feeling better. The meds are working. They have already taken a lot of stress off your heart."

She was so positive, strong, and capable, and she was telling me what I needed to hear.

She stepped out into the hall and made some calls. She decided to work remotely today so she could be with me at the hospital.

Cindy must have established a tag team, because the moment she stepped out of the room, Emmy walked in.

She looked so serious that I joked with her and said she didn't have a good reason for skipping workout. She reminded me that I was skipping workout too. She said she'd give me a pass for today, but not for much longer.

Emmy leaned forward in the chair and said, "Don't worry, you will get your strength back. You have achieved incredible goals. This is just another one of those big goals."

A nurse walked into the room and handed me a hospital gown and told me I needed to change. They would be coming to get me soon.

Emmy said she would wait in the waiting room and see me after the procedure.

I put on the gown but didn't remove my Christmas socks.

A nurse wheeled me into the room where they would do the cardioversion.

Dr. Rawal arrived a few moments later, with three assistants. Dr. Rawal said they were going to give me something to swallow to numb my throat because the tube they used could irritate it. I would be lightly sedated, but he asked me not to resist him putting the tube down my throat.

One of Dr. Rawal's assistants put a round ball, the size of a large marble, of the numbing agent on a tongue depressor. It looked like Vaseline.

He wiped the depressor against my tongue and told me to swallow it.

I tried, but it was large and cold, and it felt like I was swallowing a huge ball of snot. I gagged. I tried again and gagged harder. It was a good thing I didn't have any food in my stomach. I was embarrassed and apologized, but I couldn't get it down.

One of the assistants warned, "She has a strong gag reflex."

I have a strong gag reflex because I'm a swimmer. My body has been trained to keep water out of my lungs so I don't choke.

I tried again and thought I was going to throw up. Tears filled my eyes. I tried again.

Dr. Rawal put his hand on my shoulder. He said it was okay. I didn't have to swallow the stuff.

I don't remember being sedated, and I don't know what happened during the procedure, or what happened after.

Laura told me months later that when she saw Dr. Rawal as he came out of the cardioversion room he told her, "We tried to cardiovert her, but it didn't work. We discovered that she has a severely diminished EF and I want to cath her immediately."

Laura thought things were grim; she tried not to burst into tears.

When I woke up I saw Dr. Rawal and Laura standing near the bed. They looked at me with happy faces, as if they were saying welcome back to the world.

I couldn't keep my eyes open. I kept wanting to sleep. I wanted to say, How did it go? But there was something disconnecting my thoughts from my speech. I sounded strange. I couldn't understand what I was saying. I tried again to say, How did it go? The words sounded like they were being elongated. The medications I had received to sedate me had had an amnesiac effect. All I remember was being wheeled back into the room and trying to clear my mind.

When I woke up next I asked Dr. Rawal if everything was okay and if I could go back to my workout the next morning.

He looked at me with disbelief, and he realized that I had missed something. He said I couldn't go back to working out yet. He told me that he had a friend who was a top-ranked cyclist who was having rapid heartbeats. The cyclist's EF was down to twenty. He did an angiogram on the cyclist and found that he had cardiovascular disease. They were able to bypass his diseased arteries and improve his EF. It went from twenty to forty-five percent (not quite normal). He wasn't racing again but was still riding long distances.

"That's good," I said.

He told me I needed an angiogram.

I asked if he would be the one to do the procedure.

He said he would.

Everything was happening quickly. It seemed as though things were urgent.

Two nurses rushed into the room, detached the IV, and wheeled me in the bed through the hallway.

A nurse met us at the room where they did the angiograms. She wrapped me in a heated blanket. Another nurse asked if I had ever had an angiogram before. I said no. She recognized my name and asked if I was the open-water swimmer. She had worked in the same medical group as my dad. The other nurse had read about my swims for years. They told me not to worry. They would take good care of me. They adjusted my pillow and made sure the blanket was warm enough.

They asked what had happened to me.

I told them that I had taken care of my parents for many years, and that I was supposed to spread my mom's and dog's ashes in a couple of days. I missed them.

The nurse who knew my dad said to the other nurse, "I bet she has broken heart syndrome."

The other nurse agreed.

Laura and Charlie walked into the room.

Charlie was a retired internist, but he stayed current. He read medical journals, spoke with colleagues, and read newsletters from prominent medical schools. He had the cheeriest personality of anyone I had ever known and he was so positive that he walked with a bounce in his step.

He seemed happier than usual. I realized that he was being upbeat to allay my fears and Laura's.

They would be in the waiting room during the procedure and they would talk with Dr. Rawal as soon as they could.

Dr. Rawal was ready.

My heart beat faster.

I told myself to relax; all I had to do was breathe and sleep.

When Dr. Rawal stepped out after the procedure, Laura noticed that he had a grim look on his face.

Laura told me later that he explained to her that I had a nonischemic cardiomyopathy—heart failure that wasn't due to coronary artery disease—and that there was a chance that this could be due to a tachycardia-induced cardiomyopathy, a weak heart caused by a chronic elevated heart rate. My ejection fraction, the amount of blood my heart pumped with one beat, was critically low. Normal EF was fifty-five to sixty-five percent. My EF was between fifteen and twenty percent, consistent with someone who is dying. He would need to manage my condition aggressively with medications and consider referring me to a heart transplant center for evaluation. He said I might need to have a defibrillator put in after he had gotten me on the right medications. He thought I was at a high risk for fatal arrhythmias. The defibrillator might prevent that.

"What's the prognosis?" Laura asked.

"It's poor, but we will have a better idea when we see whether she is responding to medical therapy," he said. He looked grave.

Laura went home and burst into tears and told her brother that she thought I was going to die.

As I woke up Dr. Rawal and his team were talking about the swims I had done. One man said he wished he was a better swimmer. A nurse said she wished she was more comfortable in the water. I said I would be happy to help them swim. We could go into the ocean one day when I got out of the hospital. Their faces went blank and no one knew what to say.

Wow, I thought, they must think that I will never be able to swim again. I didn't know that they were thinking that I might die.

Dr. Rawal said I needed to stay another day in the hospital so they could continue to increase my medications and measure my response. The medications would slow my heart rate and allow my heart to rest with the hope of giving it a chance to recover. We would see how I was doing the following morning, and if things were okay, he would have me start taking the same medications on a daily basis. If I responded favorably, he would continue to increase the doses of the medicines until I reached the optimal therapeutic levels.

He said there were many different options for heart medications. "If one of those doesn't work, we can put you on the heart transplant list. I have good friends at UCLA."

He had brought that up before, but I hadn't been able to even think about it then. This time it registered. Oh my God. I don't want my heart cut out of my body. I don't want my heart taken away from me. It's my heart. It's the heart I was born with. It's the heart that's been with me through my life. It's the heart that I've loved with, hoped with, believed with. It's the heart that's given me courage. It carried me to distant shores. It's been strong. It's kept my body strong. It's the reason I've endured. I don't want to live without my heart. I don't want someone else's heart. I want mine.

Oh God, why do I have to go through this now? It isn't fair. I did all the right things. I was the good daughter. I took care of my folks for all of my adult life. I did what was expected and more. I put my desires aside for them. I know they helped me, and I helped them, but now it's my turn to live. Please let me keep the heart you gave me. Please let me keep the heart I've loved with. Please help me heal my heart. I want to live. I want to have a life.

I still want an evening in Paris, a week in Italy. I want

to sail to the North Cape in Norway, swim in Finland, hike in the Himalayas. I still want to see and do things I've never done. I want my friends and family to know that I love them, that they have made my life rich, exciting, fascinating, and happy. And I still want to fall in love and be with a man who loves me as I love him. I want more time, more life, more.

"Do you have any questions?" Dr. Rawal asked. He looked at me. His face was compassionate.

"Can I go back to my workout tomorrow morning?"

He looked at me as if I didn't understand how sick I was. I don't think I did. He didn't know that working out was like breathing to me.

He said I needed to take a few weeks off.

"Dr. Rawal, I just want to tell you, I appreciate all that you've done for me. Thank you," I said.

He smiled and said, "You're welcome."

He told me he was going to increase the medications. They would help my heart pump better. He told me that the medications might make me dizzy so I needed to stand up slowly.

I lay back in the bed and looked at the heart monitor.

My brother, sister, and sister-in-law walked into the room. They had come to the family home to scatter my mom's ashes, celebrate her life, and settle the estate. They hadn't expected to see me in the hospital. I had always been strong and healthy, the one people depended on. They weren't sure what to say or do. My brother said that I looked good. They didn't understand. I didn't look sick.

I said that I was feeling better. I seemed to be responding to the medications and if everything went well, the doctor said I could leave in the morning.

My brother offered to give me a ride home and said he hoped I would be out soon.

I remembered to call Joe the fireman. It was so good to hear his voice. He had been wondering how I was doing. I said I was sorry that it had taken me so long to call, but a lot had happened.

He was talking to me, but at the same time he was trying to work through my situation. He was explaining about the electrical conductivity of the heart and the cells within the heart and how they regulate the heartbeat. He was trying to figure out what had gone wrong.

"What's your ejection fraction?" he asked.

When I told him, he asked me to repeat it. He was at a loss for words. And when I told him that I might need a heart transplant, he couldn't believe it.

He was struggling, trying to reassure me. At the same time, he was trying to absorb the information and make sense of it.

He asked me a lot of questions I couldn't answer. He couldn't figure out why the cardioversion hadn't worked. He did cardioversions on his EMT patients and they often worked. Why hadn't it worked for me?

I didn't know. And it was better that I didn't know what Dr. Rawal thought. It would have been too much to deal with.

9

DECEMBER 21—WALKING

Emmy came by in the morning. She looked more like her normal self. She told me that it had been a long time since I was up and moving. I needed to stretch my legs, and she offered to take me on a walk. She told me to take my time.

It was difficult to keep the wheels of the IV cart in a straight line. My legs felt weak and I wobbled, but Emmy walked beside me ready to stabilize me if I started to fall. I felt strange, but I was breathing at half the rate I had been breathing when I was admitted, and I wasn't exhausted after walking two hundred meters of the cardiac wing.

We turned the corner and walked a little faster. She smiled and told me not to do too much too fast.

In every hospital room were gray-haired men and women lying in beds and connected to IVs and heart monitors. No one was visiting them. I hoped they weren't alone. I hoped they had people who cared about them. It made all the difference in getting better. I was lucky.

The farther we walked, the more the stiffness and soreness left my body. For the first time in more than a month, my lungs felt like they were fully inflating. It felt so good to be able to take deep breaths.

Each time I took a breath oxygen was pulled in and the hemoglobin in my blood carried it throughout my body. It was essential for cell metabolism and for physiological functioning. It felt good to take a deep breath, but it didn't feel normal. My breathing and heartbeat felt out of sync. Before, my heartbeat and breathing were rapid, but now my breaths were long and deep yet my heart was still beating faster than normal.

I told myself I just needed to give myself time and everything would be back in sync.

Emmy walked beside me. We had known each other for nine or ten years and worked out together five days a week at the gym. We motivated, inspired, praised, joked with, and pushed each other during our workouts and in life.

We increased our pace in the hall.

"You're much better than you were a couple of days ago." Emmy was relieved.

"Hope I can be back in the gym soon," I said.

"So do I. I miss working out with my buddy," she said.

Emmy had to leave for work, but Cindy Palin entered the room a few minutes later. The tag team was at work.

Cindy's face was more relaxed, and the warmth in her

brown eyes had returned. She sat down and asked me for today's plan.

If Dr. Rawal cleared me, I would be leaving by noon. I would have to continue taking heart medications probably for the remainder of my life. I wasn't thrilled about that.

Cindy was practical. She said the medications would help me recover and taking them was a lot better than any of the alternatives. She had a way of analyzing any situation and amplifying the positive.

I told her that I didn't want a lot of people to know that I was ill. Someone had called Greg, a friend, and told him that I was in the hospital. Greg misinterpreted what he was told and thought I had had a heart attack and was going to die.

We had known each other since we were teenagers and I had always been strong. He couldn't comprehend that I could be weak. He couldn't imagine me being in the hospital. He was shocked. No matter what I told him, he was inconsolable.

I realized that I didn't have the energy to explain to other friends about my heart. It took too much away from me. I needed to focus that energy on myself so I could get well.

A moment later, Sandy Field walked into the room. She looked uncomfortable.

"Hey, looks like it's time for a party," I said.

Sandy smiled.

We had had years of fun together. She was the friend who encouraged me to join her in Costa Rica at Thanksgiving. She handed me a basket of beautiful blueberries, raspberries, and strawberries.

They smelled good, and they were plump and sweet, the best berries I had ever tasted.

When Dr. Rawal entered the room, he looked much happier. He said that the medications were working. My heart was more stable and I was doing better. He was going to release me.

I was elated. My care had been fantastic, but I couldn't wait to get home, shower, and get some sleep.

Dr. Rawal said he wanted me to follow up with him in a week at his office.

I asked him why I needed to do that. I thought I could go home and I would get better.

He looked to see if I was joking and realized I wasn't. He needed to see me in a week to see how I was adjusting to the medications. I still didn't realize how ill I was.

He wanted me to monitor my blood pressure, heart rate, and weight daily. He prescribed more Lasix and said it would cause me to drop ten to twelve pounds of fluid that I had retained because of my poor cardiac output.

I decided to keep a journal like I did when I was training for a channel swim. That would allow me to track my progress. I needed to be consistent, just as I was for my training. To get consistent readings I would measure my blood pressure and heart rate every morning before

I climbed out of bed. I would measure my weight every morning before I got dressed. If my weight increased by three pounds in three days, my cardiac output was not good. I needed to take more Lasix.

Too much salt in my diet would increase water retention. Dr. Rawal advised me not to eat more than 2,000 milligrams of sodium a day. He said most people found it difficult to reduce their salt intake to that level, but I decided to keep it below 1,000 milligrams. If I could adjust my diet and reduce the salt, I might be able to stop taking the Lasix and that would reduce stress on my kidneys. That would be one less medication I would have to take. I wanted to figure out how I could get to a point where I didn't need any medications.

He asked if I had any questions.

My mother's ashes were going to be released into the ocean tomorrow by family and friends. Could I swim out and release them?

Again Dr. Rawal looked at me with disbelief, but he asked me how far I needed to swim and how cold the water would be.

The swim would only be a mile and a half (2.4 kilometers), and the water temperature would be about 55 degrees Fahrenheit (12.8 degrees centigrade). I hadn't been in the ocean for a while, but I thought I would be okay.

"Only a mile and a half?" Dr. Rawal said, and shook his head. He was a runner, and so he couldn't imagine swimming a mile and a half, but I was a swimmer and couldn't imagine running a mile and a half.

He said it was dangerous for me to swim. The penetration site in my femoral artery for the angiogram was not completely healed. It might open and I might bleed out into the ocean.

Bleeding out wasn't good. And I thought the blood in the water might attract sharks, and that wouldn't be safe for me and the rest of the family.

Dr. Rawal also told me that he didn't want me to lift anything heavy.

"Can I carry my swim bag out of the hospital?" I asked.

"How much does it weigh?" he asked.

"Not much. Maybe fifteen pounds."

He lifted the bag with both hands and said it was too heavy.

He explained: "Heavy lifting stresses the heart, and in your condition I would like you to refrain from any strenuous activities."

I nodded.

He asked if I had other questions.

I said I was planning to visit friends in New York City and in upstate New York from December 27 through January 6. Would it be okay to travel?

He said I could go but that I needed to make sure to get a travel bag with wheels. He said that I had to make sure not to lift the bag into the overhead bin because the penetration site for the angiogram could open and start bleeding. He said if that happened to apply heavy pressure to the site and hold it until you get medical attention. He also advised me to get up and walk around the aircraft to make sure I didn't get a blood clot.

If something went wrong during the trip, did he have colleagues he could refer me to? He told me to call him if I had any problems. He would be able to refer me to cardiologists in New York City. He needed to make his rounds, but he would stop by before I left to make sure everything was okay. The nurse would be in soon with discharge papers.

I called Joe to let him know I was going home. He couldn't understand how a world-class athlete could have an ejection fraction of only fifteen to twenty. He wondered why my heart cells weren't firing in sequence.

"Could it be from the cardiomyopathy?"

"Yes, your heart is stretched out of shape; the cells are not in their normal position in the heart and they aren't able to fire in their normal sequence. That makes sense. You just need to get your heart back to its normal shape. The meds will take the load off so it will rest, but there's more you can do. I need to do some research and get back to you," he said.

"Sounds good."

"What are you doing next?"

"Going home and sleeping."

"Can you call me or text me when you're home so I know you're there safely?"

"Yes, thank you, Joe. You're a great friend."

"Is there anything else you want to talk about before you head home?" he asked. There was one thing that had been really bothering me.

I told Joe about a friend who had come to visit, and how she was angry with me for not letting her know what was wrong.

He said that she was afraid for me. When people are sick, their loved ones are struggling with the illness too. He said that I needed to be gentle with her and reassure her that I was going to be okay. That would help her be less afraid.

I changed into my street clothes and sat on the edge of the bed and waited to be discharged.

A nurse walked into the room and removed the IV from my hand. She held my hand, pressed the incision site firmly with gauze, and stuck a Band-Aid on top. She continued holding my hand. She said she was praying for me.

I thanked her and she said she prayed I would survive. She looked somber.

I asked her why she was praying for me.

"Your EF is only twelve to fifteen. Most people with an ejection fraction that low die. I'm praying that God will keep you alive," she said.

"Thank you for your prayers," I said. But I thought, As a nurse she wasn't supposed to tell me that.

Dr. Rawal returned to the room. He said he needed

to listen to my heart one more time before I could go. He smiled and said my heart was beating slower and the meds were working.

I wasn't sure if I should say anything, but what the nurse told me really troubled me.

I told him what the nurse said to me.

"Your ejection fraction is low," he agreed.

It seemed surreal to ask him this, but I had to.

"Can I expect to live a month or two or should I plan to live longer?"

He touched my shoulder and said, "You should plan on living longer."

"Okay," I said.

He gave me hope. I could do a lot with that. Hope was what I used to carry me across vast channels. Hope was what allowed me to find the possible within the impossible. Hope was what gave me the courage to reach deeper and try harder and reach distant shores.

10

DECEMBER 22—DRIFTING AWAY

The next afternoon, friends and a couple of neighbors walked with me to the end of Seal Beach Pier. The wind was gusting, puffy white clouds were sailing across an aqua blue sky. The sun was strong. The sea was in motion, vibrant and alive.

My siblings and their partners gathered on the beach, put on wet suits, and swam parallel to the pier with our mom's and Cody's ashes.

I leaned into the cold wind and waited at the end of the pier for the ceremony to start.

My mom would have loved this blustery day. She would have loved to compose an abstract painting using the colors of sea, the pure white of the surf, the colors of the sun, clouds, and bright fishermen's clothes on the pier. She would have loved sketching the fluid shapes of the moving water and incorporating textures in the waves, sand, wooden pier, and sky. She loved listening to the music of the ocean and the voices of family and friends.

A friend handed me a long-stemmed dark red rose. It reminded me of Mom, so beautiful and deep.

I looked at the ocean. She loved water. She loved to swim and gave me her love of water and her love of life. I missed her so much. And I missed Cody.

My siblings and their partners swam beyond Seal Beach Pier and formed a circle. They released Cody's ashes and then they released our mother's ashes.

There were bits of conversations carried to us on the pier, and laughter. We watched the family sip merlot from a bottle and pass it around the circle. I thanked God for my mom, and all that she had given me in my life. I tossed the red rose into the ocean. It fell and floated on silvery blue waves and bobbed in the sunlight.

My heart was breaking.

"Good-bye, Cody. Good-bye, Mom. I will always love you," I whispered.

The wind blew my tears into the ocean toward the ashes.

I hoped they were okay.

11

DECEMBER 23—IN THE ARMS OF FRIENDS

After saying good-bye, friends drove me home, and I went to bed. I wasn't feeling well. My siblings arrived later with extended family and friends. It had been my home, but everything had changed. My siblings had started sorting through the things they would take and they would soon be leaving.

Cindy Palin dropped by to see how I was doing. She took one look at me and said, "Pack your bags, you're coming home with me." She knew I was planning to spend Christmas with Laura and Charlie and then leave for New York City. She told me to pack a second bag so I could leave from Laura's for New York. She would plan on picking me up at the airport when I returned.

She carried my bags to the car and into the guest room at her home and told me to rest while she made dinner for us. She gave me a hug, and I fought back the tears.

"Cindy, I'm afraid I might die," I said.

Cindy looked shocked and afraid, but she regained her

composure and reminded me how far I'd come. Two days ago I was in dire straits, and now I was better. She told me to give the medications time to work. Dr. Rawal did not know me like she did. He did not know what I was capable of achieving.

"You've swum in Antarctica in just a swimsuit in thirty-two-degree water. I don't know anyone else in the world who could do that."

"I don't know anyone else who would want to," I joked.

She told me to put my feet up and rest.

I was weary to the bone. She knew what I was feeling. She had cared for her mother, grandmother, and aunt. Within a few months she lost them all.

I fell asleep and dreamed that Cindy and I had a slumber party and her grandmother came to visit us. She wanted to make sure we were happy and strong, and she reminded us to enjoy each day. She said she couldn't stay long; she had to return to heaven to visit with my mom.

When I woke up I realized I hadn't called Joe. I needed to touch base with him and listen to his suggestions. He had been badly injured a number of times during his career as a firefighter, and he had seen his buddies suffer from physical and mental trauma. Through those experiences, Joe learned how to recover and how to support his friends during their recoveries. His knowledge wasn't theoretical. It was something he learned by going through the process himself.

He reminded me of my Olympic swimming coach. He knew when to support and encourage, and when to push.

He was strong and certain, and I felt weak and indecisive.

He explained that I had been in a crisis situation and I was making a transition. I needed to change my inner dialogue—the things I was telling myself were negative. I needed to change and talk to myself in a positive way.

My negative thinking had produced stress hormones that affected my heart. I needed to think positive and be happy so my heart would heal.

He said the connection between my heart and mind was incredibly strong. That connection allowed me to accomplish extraordinary physical and mental feats. Things no one else could imagine or do. The mind-body connection that I had developed was rare. I had used a positive mind-set to achieve my goals, but somehow my thinking pattern had changed. I needed to purge the negative thoughts, rewire my mind, and focus on a positive outcome for my heart.

The things he said made sense, and the way he told me what he thought was delivered gently, and I knew he was doing all he could to support me.

I didn't want to be negative, but I told him that I felt so weak, depleted, and vulnerable. Whatever anyone said to me, I took to heart. And that amplified my emotional response.

It was difficult to be positive when I felt awful. I wasn't

accustomed to feeling like this and couldn't shake the negative thoughts.

Joe told me I needed to focus on what I could do and the things that were working. He reminded me of the channels I had crossed and the things I had achieved. He asked me questions about what I had done, things I had never written or spoken about, so I would focus on the memories and tell him the things I had done to overcome huge obstacles and achieve those goals. He told me to focus on those experiences and remember who I was so I would find myself again.

Joe's voice became soft. "Do you know what heals the human heart?" he asked.

"What heals the human heart?" I asked him.

"Love," he said.

My eyes filled with tears. That was it. That was what this part of my life's journey was about. It was love. Love from the people who loved me and the people I loved. Love was what healed the human heart. It was what was healing my heart.

12

THE GIFT

It was the first Christmas Eve I would spend without my mom. In the later years of her life, I made Christmas dinner and we celebrated with friends, or we joined Laura and Charlie for their family gathering. I couldn't help but think about my mom.

Christmas was her favorite holiday. She grew up in a family that began wrapping their Christmas gifts in June. She had five aunts, two uncles, and grandparents who owned a design store in Waterville, Maine. They sold wallpaper, paint, and fabric and designed interiors and exteriors of homes and offices.

They used the remnants to decorate the packages, and as soon as Christmas was over, they began thinking about what they would give one another the next Christmas and how they would design the packages.

My mom lived for Christmas. She loved to decorate our home, tree, and presents. She loved to sit beside the tree and just look at it.

It was strange. I wouldn't be home. She wouldn't be

watching me cook and advising me on the best way to make her special recipes. She wasn't there to laugh with me.

But I was with Laura and Charlie and we were making seven desserts for Christmas Eve. We would be driving to Howard's, Laura's brother's, home to have dinner with the family.

We baked and talked all day. Each time the oven opened, the kitchen was filled with waves of warmth and smells of chocolate, cinnamon, roasted raisins, toasted walnuts, nutmeg, baked almonds, vanilla, and cardamom.

When the last dessert was in the oven, I sat down in a recliner and put my feet up.

Charlie walked over to me and asked, "Are you okay?"

I was happy and just relaxing for a moment before we started frosting the cake. "I'm a little tired," I admitted.

"You look better than you did a couple days ago," he said.

"No one looks good in those hospital gowns," I said.

"You're right." He grinned.

Just being with them made me happy and that made me feel better.

"Laura has something she wants to tell you," he said.

"We've done a lot of research and we think you have broken heart syndrome."

Dr. Rawal said that my heart problem was idiopathic—its cause was unknown. But Laura and Charlie thought they had discovered what I had.

"The American Heart Association says that broken

heart syndrome is caused by an emotionally stressful event. It can be caused by the death of a loved one, a divorce, a romantic rejection, a breakup, a physical separation, or a betrayal. Your mom's death and releasing her ashes were stressful for you," Laura said.

She didn't know that there were two more stressors that affected my heart. A friend whom I was interested in told me he was seeing someone else, and another friend was moving away. He had a new job and I didn't know if I would ever see him again. It seemed like my life was only about loss. Life was too sad.

"When someone has broken heart syndrome, part of the heart suddenly enlarges due to extreme stress. Dr. Rawal found that the ventricle in the lower part of your heart was enlarged. The Japanese doctor who discovered broken heart syndrome called it takotsubo cardiomyopathy. 'Takotsubo' is the Japanese word fishermen use for octopus traps. The octopus traps' shape resembles the enlarged ventricle," Charlie explained, and drew a heart on a napkin that showed the enlarged ventricle and then he drew an octopus trap. They looked the same.

Charlie said the other symptoms of broken heart syndrome were arrhythmias and cardiogenic shock.

"What is cardiogenic shock?" I asked.

"Cardiogenic shock is a condition that occurs when a weakened heart can't pump enough blood to meet the body's need. That's what happened to you. Your heart was too weak to pump blood effectively."

"It was an emergency situation, like a heart attack?" I asked.

"Yes. With broken heart syndrome some people have a sudden intense pain in the chest caused by a surge of stress hormones, and it can feel like a heart attack. But you didn't experience this symptom."

"It's a good thing you sent me to see a cardiologist," I said.

Laura and Charlie shifted uncomfortably.

"We talked about it and think it may have been better to send you to emergency, but we wanted you to be seen by someone we knew."

"Dr. Rawal took good care of me. I'm glad you referred me to him," I said.

"I don't think you would be alive if you hadn't seen him," Laura said with tightness in her voice. "I hope you don't mind, but I called another friend who is a cardiologist to confirm Dr. Rawal's treatment."

She said her cardiologist friend was about to retire. I had met him at one of Laura's dinner parties. He invented a part for the medical device that was used for angiograms. He told Laura he agreed with Dr. Rawal's treatment method and that giving me medications that made my heart rest would allow it to heal.

"The best news is that you can completely recover from broken heart syndrome," Laura said.

I never thought I would be happy to have a broken heart, but now I was. I took a deep breath.

"Do you think I will recover?" I asked.

"I'm sure you will. You agree, don't you, Charlie?" Laura asked.

"I do. I think she will fully recover," he said.

"What an amazing gift you have given me this Christmas," I said to them. I felt a new sense of gratitude and a deeper sense of love for them and for my friends. I realized how fortunate I was to have their love and support.

Laura and Charlie had been thinking a lot about my condition and they said that I needed to reduce my stress.

They decided to take me to a meditation course at UCLA, so I could learn new ways to meditate and reduce my stress, and they said they were available for me anytime.

13

CHRISTMAS EVE AT HOWARD'S

We drove to Howard's to celebrate Christmas Eve. Family and friends were arriving in small groups, and everyone was dressed up for the celebration.

Adults I had known as children were holding their children on their laps. The children's eyes were bright and they were so excited it was Christmas. They couldn't wait to open gifts. The adults felt their energy and excitement too. Everyone was happy.

Love was simmering in the kitchen, and it smelled delicious. There were seven fishes being prepared: calamari cooking in a pot of red wine, garlic, onion, and tomato sauce; anchovies baking in bread rolls in the oven; baccalà, salted codfish in spicy red pepper tomato sauce simmering in a deep saucepan; king salmon sprinkled with olive oil, parsley, and lemon baking in the oven; and a tray of shiny sardines in oil, thin slices of bright orange lox, and pickled herring with onions, vinegar, and sugar being arranged on platters.

On a side table was a platter of heirloom tomatoes and burrata cheese, bowls of black and green olives and sweet and dill pickles, slices of yellow cheddar and white provolone cheese, tortilla chips, fresh guacamole, salsa, ruffled potato chips, and onion dip. There were trays of fresh chopped carrots, celery, cucumbers, and cherry tomatoes and ranch dressing.

On another table were Christmas cookies—stars, Santa Clauses, and reindeers sprinkled with bright red, white, and green sugar—and thick-frosted cakes and glistening pies.

Everything looked exquisite and smelled delicious. I wanted to try a little of everything like I always did at Christmas. But everything was full of salt, especially the baccalà.

It was depressing. I couldn't have what I wanted to eat. But I thought, What's more important, eating what you want or keeping your heart healthy?

I needed to think about food in a different way. I needed to figure out what I could eat and enjoy it, rather than focusing on what I couldn't have. I could eat the baked salmon; I loved salmon. I could eat the raw vegetables— the cooked vegetables had been salted and I had no idea how much salt had been added. The cheeses, chips, dips, and olives were full of salt. I could shell the raw walnuts and eat them, and I could eat the fresh fruit for dessert. I would adjust.

We lined up, filled our plates, and sat at the long table

and listened to family stories about Christmas Eves past. We got up and changed seats so we could sit beside other family members and talk. Laura and Charlie sat beside me.

Howard made a few funny comments about himself and Laura, and he made me laugh.

Laura said she was happy that I was laughing again. She told me laughter was good for my heart. It released good hormones and made my heart feel good.

I told her I was happy I was there.

Laura's eyes filled with tears. "Glad you're here too," she said and hugged me.

We opened Christmas gifts from youngest to oldest, and it seemed like each person was as excited about giving his or her gifts as receiving them.

The evening passed too quickly. We walked outside to say good night. The air was cold and the sky was so clear we could see the constellations. The stars were sparkling like white, blue, and yellow diamonds. It was amazing to look up and see the universe and know we were a part of it.

We gazed at the moon. It was bright. Howard pointed out Mars and Venus.

One adult asked the children if they could see Santa and his reindeer flying across the sky.

The children stared at the sky, searching. They leaned back and looked into the heavens.

Someone said he thought he saw Santa, and the children did not want to leave until they did too.

The children were reluctantly climbing into the cars when Howard shouted and pointed, "Look, a shooting star."

We watched the star make a wide blazing white arc across the black sky.

It seemed like a little miracle.

"It's a Christmas star," a boy shouted. His voice was filled with awe.

"Did you make wish?" a girl asked.

"Yes, I did," he said.

"Did you?" he asked me.

"Yes, I made a wish," I said.

14

NEW YORK CITY AND THE COUNTRY

The baking and cooking and feasting continued at Laura's on Christmas Day. More family and friends arrived to celebrate.

At one point, I retreated to a guest room and lay down. I was exhausted, but it was a happy exhaustion. I was learning how to slow down and relax rather than to continue pushing myself.

The party grew louder, and there was laughter, bits and pieces of conversations, and happy voices.

There was a knock on the door. It was Laura. She wanted to know if I was feeling all right.

I told her I just needed to take a break. I felt like I was getting better, but I wasn't feeling quite right. My body was out of sync.

She asked if I had checked my heart rate and blood pressure.

I took it three times because I was trying to learn how to use the blood pressure machine, and I wanted to see if there was much variation in the measurements. I waited three minutes between each test to make sure I got good readings. There was considerable variation, which surprised me, but all the readings were low. I was fine.

She wanted to make sure I was okay and offered to send Charlie to see me.

Charlie knocked on the door and said that Laura was a little worried about me. I could tell he was too. He asked if I was feeling heart palpitations—skipped or accelerated heartbeats. Was I short of breath or dizzy?

I didn't have any symptoms, I just didn't feel normal. I thought I just needed a break and said I would be back downstairs soon.

His face relaxed and he left the room with a bounce in his step.

I closed my eyes and fell asleep. When I woke up it was morning. Laura was already up making breakfast. She had checked on me before she went to bed, and Charlie did too.

I laughed and thanked her. I felt like a little kid, but I was so lucky they cared that much.

We visited with family and friends all day, and I was leaving for New York City the next morning. Usually I was excited about going there, but now I wasn't sure if I wanted to go. I felt physically unstable and unsure.

Checking my e-mail before I left, I noticed one from Joe with good advice. He said that I was going to have a long trip and I needed to hydrate during the flight, and take walking breaks, and prefly the emotional trip to make it go the way I wanted. He wrote, "Like a plane has a compass heading, you need a positive outcome focus point. There will be stupid thoughts trying to suck up some of your emotional energy. When that comes up, think about you, who you are, what you've accomplished, the best is yet to come, what a great vacation you are about to have. Take a deep breath, sigh, and just grin, buddy, one big grin! Those thoughts will vaporize away."

When Laura hugged me there were tears in her eyes.

"I'll be fine. Don't worry," I said, and I felt my eyes fill with tears. I was never this emotional.

She told me to take good care and stay in touch. Charlie hugged me.

It was strange traveling without my swim bag. It always went with me. I would sling it over my shoulder and carry it and a small bag onto the airplane. It was a simple way to travel.

But the bag was too heavy for me to carry. A friend lent me her small travel bag with wheels.

When I climbed onto the JetBlue flight I opened the overhead compartment and felt awkward. I always packed and carried my own gear, but the incision site for the angiogram wasn't completely healed. If I tried to lift the bag, it could open and bleed.

A man around my age, sitting in a seat behind mine, jumped to his feet. He asked if I needed help.

I felt so lame.

He lifted my bag with one hand like he was Superman and stowed it in the compartment.

I thanked him.

When the plane landed at JFK, before I could ask for help, the man set the bag down beside me and handed it to me with the handle. I thanked him again.

"My pleasure," he said.

I was surprised. He was happy to help. It was nice.

They say Paris is the City of Lights, but during the holiday season, New York City rivals Paris. The lights on Broadway, above Times Square, in Rockefeller Plaza, and on boats sailing the Hudson River shone brighter than I remembered. The city was filled with holiday cheer, and there was magic in the air.

Martha Kaplan welcomed me into her apartment. She invited me to go with her to her country home and to spend time with good friends: Vicky Wilson, my editor; Kathy Hourigan, my managing editor; and Andy Hughes, the person in charge of production, would be joining us to celebrate the New Year. Martha said it would be good for me to get away and be with friends.

We drove to the country along snowy roads with Frankie, her happy black-and-white spotted dog. Her old farmhouse was so cold that we could see our steamy white breath. It didn't take long for the downstairs area to grow warm once the heater was turned on. Martha carried my luggage up dark wooden steps to the guest room and she told me to sleep as long as I wanted. I followed slowly, not wanting to make my heart work too hard.

I slept for fourteen hours. I realized I had not slept that well in years.

Martha was having friends over for New Year's Day, but I was too tired to help. I felt like I had instantly become an old person.

Martha told me not to worry and to sleep as long as I wanted.

Pushing away all thoughts, I relaxed and slept again for almost twenty-four hours, woke up, drank a couple glasses of water, ate an apple, and slept for twelve more.

Martha couldn't believe how much I slept.

Long, thick icicles hung in clusters from the eaves of the house. The earth was covered with a thick blanket of snow and the bright sunshine made the snow crystals sparkle like a billion stars.

The snow was hard, and it crunched and squeaked when I walked. A breeze blowing across the wide fields lifted the chill into the air and made it colder.

I walked into the breeze and felt the enormous contrast between the warmth of my body and the icy air. Cold air splashed against my face and slid into my lungs. It cleared my groggy mind. The cold air and the warmth within my body felt like a contrast between death and life. I walked a little faster to get warmer and gazed across the snowy fields.

The area was used for dairy cattle, but there weren't any cows. It was too cold for them.

The wind increased and lifted the snow in whirling

sheets. Birch and maple branches encased in ice clattered, and loud calls from ravens filled the air. They were in the tall pine trees down the road. They shared their food in winter. They scanned the ground until one signaled with a loud caw. The flock suddenly launched and flew along the dark winding road.

It began to snow. Delicate snow crystals stuck to my eyelashes and melted on my face.

The wind gusted, and cold cut through my wool scarf. I walked toward Andy's house, up the road from Martha's. Smoke was rising from his chimney and the air was filled with the sweet smell of burning wood. If it started snowing harder or grew colder, I would knock on his door and visit with him and thaw.

Something was missing. It was his stream. In spring, summer, and fall it sang with the flow of the season. The stream was frozen now. Large air bubbles were trapped in the ice. It looked like the stream had frozen in midbreath. In spring the stream would flow and the air bubbles would be freed into the air. I wondered if I would live until spring.

Crossing the road, I walked into the forest and remembered lines from Robert Frost's poem "Stopping by Woods on a Snowy Evening."

The woods are lovely, dark and deep,
But I have promises to keep,
And miles to go before I sleep,
And miles to go before I sleep.

The woods were lovely, dark and deep, and I had things I still wanted to do. I had miles to go before I slept. Until now I had thought I would have time to go those miles, but now I wasn't sure.

We gathered at Vicky's home for New Year's Eve. She had a house nearby where she worked, edited, swam, and rode horses.

Vicky is my editor and I was so lucky to find her. She helped me live my dream of being an author, guided and edited my work, and helped me clarify my thoughts. She is smart, honest, and sensitive, and she has become a good friend.

Kathy Hourigan, the managing editor at Knopf, was there too. Kathy is my friend and one of the kindest and most enthusiastic people I have ever met. She loves books and stories and I love talking with her about what she is reading and editing.

We raised our glasses and toasted the New Year and good health.

Kathy and Vicky cleared the dishes, and they returned carrying a birthday cake. It was decorated with soft blue, yellow, and pink wildflowers and candles. The dessert was to celebrate the new year and my birthday a few days later. They sang "Happy Birthday," and I blew out the candles. What a year it had been. What a new year it would be.

15

SHELTERED

Cindy Palin picked me up at the airport and drove me home. The house was dark and cold. Emptier than it had ever been. I turned on the lights. Rugs, furniture, and dishes and vases my mother once loved were gone. My siblings had taken their share of the furnishings.

Cindy asked where the heat was so she could turn it on. She sat with me and listened to stories about my New York travels.

It was almost midnight, and she had to get her daughter off to school in the morning and then go to work. She told me to call her if I needed anything.

I walked through the house. It felt like my home was dying as pieces of it were carried away. I didn't want to stay for the death of my home. I needed to leave, but I couldn't do it all at once.

Friends invited me to stay with them for a few days, others invited me to move in with them for as long as I wanted, and one couple told me I was welcome to stay at their home in central California. I could have their house to myself. It was quiet, near the beach. I could get a lot of writing done. I would have loved staying with any of them, but I knew if I did I would be delaying a decision I needed to make. I needed to find a home where I could restart my life. I had not lived on my own since college, and I needed to have my own place and a new beginning.

I couldn't figure out if I wanted to buy a place or rent. My friends advised me to rent for a while. I didn't need to rush into anything, and I didn't need the pressure of owning a house. I wasn't sure if I was living or if I was dying. It never seemed so difficult to make decisions, but friends helped me. They were there for me.

I needed to get back into the gym and move and stretch and feel good again, but part of me just wanted to curl up into a comfortable ball and sleep.

My workout friend Emmy convinced me to meet her for coffee with our workout buddies. She had a plan, but she kept it to herself. She thought if she could get me to meet for coffee, the group could "baby-step" me back to the gym.

But working out was going to be difficult. I had been an elite athlete. All of that had changed in a few heartbeats.

I didn't know what I could or couldn't do. I didn't know if I wanted to know. It was frightening facing another loss. Was life about losses?

Emmy encouraged me to climb on the elliptical machine. We could program the workout.

We moved our arms and legs back and forth against a set resistance. The resistance and steepness could be increased and decreased. I used to work out at level twenty, the highest resistance and the steepest level. I had worked like an endurance athlete and used well-paced strides and arm pulls. Now I climbed on the elliptical machine and put the resistance on level one—the lowest level.

Emmy said that it was a good place to start. She began working out on her machine. She set it to level ten.

I needed to build up gradually.

Dr. Rawal advised me to monitor my heart during my workout. My heart rate when I was working at a moderate pace was 120 beats per minute. He told me to maintain a heart rate below 110 beats. If I felt light-headed, dizzy, or short of breath, I needed to stop. Part of me wanted to scream, to throw a fit, to give up. I felt so overwhelmed, controlled, and so limited. It seemed like I had to start all over again. I had prided myself on being an elite athlete, and now I had to start from zero. It was sad, sobering, and scary.

I began moving my legs slowly back and forth to wake them up and start the blood flowing. I checked my heart rate by holding the handles on the machine. The display showed my heart was beating at 100 beats per minute for a few moments. It suddenly increased to 136 and fluctuated wildly.

It was awful. I was using the lightest resistance and my heart was beating too fast and too irregularly. How much slower could I go? I had never asked myself that question. Never tried to go slow.

Everything was peculiar. Slow was good. Fast was not. Light resistance was good. Heavy resistance was not.

"You okay?" Emmy asked.

"It doesn't feel like I'm getting any workout," I said.

"Just go through the motions. So your body can move and your heart can rest."

I slowed down to one pull, one second rest, two pulls, one second rest. My heart rate continued to be between 120 and 130 beats per minute. It was too high.

What was wrong with me? I couldn't regulate my heart, couldn't keep it below 110 beats per minute. I was angry at myself. Why can't I do this? What if I can't get my heart rate down? What if I can't exercise? What if I can't be with my friends?

Nothing I was doing worked, and after being on the elliptical machine for ten minutes, I had to climb off. It was so frustrating.

"You did a great job. Tomorrow maybe you can increase your workout by a minute or two," Emmy said, and smiled.

"That would be great," I said, trying to sound positive. But I thought, You've swum across the English Channel, and now you can't swim across a puddle. This is awful.

"Want to use the rowing machine?" Emmy asked.

"Sure," I said.

We sat down and rowed side by side. She paced her

pull with mine. She pulled strongly. I used no resistance. My heartbeat was slower, probably because I was sitting down. We watched the news on televisions above our heads, commented on the stories, and rowed for twenty minutes.

My body felt better after moving, but I was far from the athlete I once was. It was depressing.

Emmy met me at the gym the next morning for our workout and handed me a birthday gift.

It was a heart monitor. She gave it to me so I could wear it and monitor my heart while we worked out. It was more accurate than the handheld heart monitor on the elliptical machine and would display continuous readings so I would know how my heart was functioning. That would allow me to adjust my workout by increasing or decreasing my pace.

I walked into the locker room, put on the monitor, adjusted the strap and sensor around my chest, put the watch that would display my heart rate around my wrist.

We climbed on the elliptical machines and I looked at the monitor. The numbers were changing more rapidly than they did on the elliptical's monitor. The display showed that my heart was beating irregularly. It beat at 146 for about ten seconds, then dropped to 90 for a few seconds, and leaped up to 140. I moved my arms and legs slowly but my heart continued beating erratically, and faster than 110 beats per minute.

It was strange; my body was functioning so differently

than it did before I was ill. I used to be able to get into my pace, and I'd felt my heart and lungs working at a constant rate. Now there was a disconnect. I wasn't working at all and my heart was working too hard.

Emmy suggested readjusting the band around my chest.

I returned to the locker room and placed the monitor in a different area. I tried exercising again, and the numbers were as erratic as before.

Emmy suggested that we leave the machines and take the spin class. If I sat and worked out, my heart rate would be lower than if I stood.

We sat on our bikes and cycled to the beat of the music. I set the tension on my bike to zero so I could spin my legs without any resistance. I told myself to relax and focus on moving my legs slowly.

I checked the monitor. My heartbeat was as erratic and fast as when I climbed a steep hill, but it wasn't pounding in my chest, and I wasn't breathless. My heart muscle was weak. It was beating ineffectively.

Emmy glanced at me. "You okay?" she asked.

I didn't know what I was. I didn't like the way I was. I didn't like what was happening to me. I didn't like that I didn't know what to do.

I stopped and tried to find a solution. I needed to stop using the heart monitor. It was making me anxious and obsessive, and that was making my heart rate increase. I would monitor myself, take my heart rate manually, monitor my breathing, and ask myself how I was feeling. If I wasn't okay, I'd slow down, and if I was, I would continue.

I placed my finger on my carotid artery and counted. My heart rate was 102 beats per minute.

"That's good," Emmy said.

"Much better," I said with great relief.

16

REWIRING THE MIND

My life was arrhythmic. I used to be able to find a rhythm. I could set a goal, align my heart and mind, overcome obstacles, and achieve whatever I wanted to do, but now I couldn't get my heart, mind, and body back into their normal rhythm.

Each day I vacillated between being hopeful and believing I could get better and being filled with despair and doubting if I ever would. It was the darkest and the most confusing time in my life.

Joe knew I was in a dark place and knew how to help me find my way out. He said that negative thoughts were like parasites. They were often transmitted from one person to another by negative comments.

These parasites had infected my head and heart when my resistance was low. They knew how to use my DNA to replicate and thrive. I needed to rewire my mind, think positively, change my DNA, rid myself of the parasites, and restore my health.

He said that in the morning when I climbed out of bed, I needed to look in the mirror and smile.

It sounded like a ridiculous thing to do, but I realized what I had been doing wasn't working for me, and I needed to change.

The next morning, I walked into the bathroom and looked at myself. What I saw shocked me. The light in my green eyes was gone. The color in my cheeks had faded and my lips were drooping. I didn't look like me anymore. Where had I gone?

I shook my head. I looked half dead.

You will be okay.

I smiled.

The light in my eyes returned, my face lifted, and the color returned. I felt ridiculous smiling at myself, but smiling made me happy.

Suddenly I remembered a passage from the Bible: *This is the day that the Lord has made; let us rejoice and be glad in it.*

I smiled again. It was a day the Lord had made. I was happy to live it.

In the evening I called Joe and told him what had happened, and I said I was smiling.

He laughed and said he could hear the warmth in my voice. I said I was surprised that smiling could make you feel better. I told him I always used to smile when I woke up in the morning. I always used to look forward to each day. I was happy because I had the whole day in front of me, and it was filled with many possibilities.

"When did you stop smiling?" he asked.

"When I was caring for my parents I woke up each morning and wondered if they were still alive or if they had died during the night. I dreaded checking on them."

"Have you spoken with anyone about this?" he asked.

"Never thought of it before this conversation, but things have changed. My parents are in a better place, and I can wake up in the morning and smile."

"That's right," he said.

He worked with me like a coach and built upon what he taught me. He said anytime I saw my reflection in a mirror, or a window, anywhere I needed to smile.

"What are people going to think if they see me smiling at myself?"

"Who cares what they think. The reason you're smiling is because it makes you feel better," he said.

Joe asked me to tell him a joke.

He said that I needed to tell jokes because laughter releases endorphins, and they make you feel better. Laughter temporarily relieves pain, boosts your immune system, and improves blood flow to your heart. When you're laughing you aren't stressed.

He asked me if I had seen any comedies recently.

I was only watching spy thrillers and mysteries.

He shared his favorites with me and recounted some of his favorite scenes from the Pink Panther movies, Monty Python, and *Young Frankenstein*.

We laughed hard. It felt good to laugh.

I told him I saw the movie *Up* and loved it. The beginning was beautiful and sad. Two kids became best friends, grew up, married, and shared an adventurous dream. The wife died before she could fulfill the dream, but the husband carried their dream forward when he befriended a young boy and a dog.

"I don't want to see it," Joe said.

"But it's sweet and inspiring," I said.

"Do you know how many times I've had to tell people that their loved ones have died? Do you know what it's like to see their faces when I tell them? I don't want to see a sad movie," he said, sighing.

He had seen too much and I had felt too much.

"Make sure you don't watch the news or anything else horrible or depressing before you go to sleep. Those thoughts can enter the subconscious at a time when your resistance to negative thoughts is low. You need to meditate before you sleep and make it part of your evening routine. You also need to listen to music that you like. It will make you feel happy. Sleep well," he said.

"You too, buddy," I said.

The next morning I walked into spin class and started laughing. The room was covered with mirrors from floor to ceiling. I smiled.

Emmy glanced at me and smiled. She sat beside me. Another friend sat beside Emmy. She saw Emmy and she smiled. A friend across the room glanced in the mirror and saw us smiling. She smiled.

A woman sitting near me smiled and asked, "Having a good day today?"

"I am," I said.

The instructor saw us and smiled. She turned the music up and climbed on her bicycle and started spinning.

The class matched our pace to hers. We warmed up. The class sped up. I moved my legs slowly and felt my pulse. My heart was beating at one hundred beats per minute. I could go faster. It was great.

I heard Bruce Springsteen singing "It's My Life," and I sang along: "It's my life and I'll do what I want. It's my mind and I'll think what I want."

The music changed and Pink sang about love and life and I sang along: "You've gotta get up and try and try and try. Gotta get up and try and try and try." I was getting up and trying and trying and trying. It felt like I was starting to find my rhythm.

17

JANUARY 19, 2013—JOY AND INSPIRATION

Jay Movius called. He was one of the friends I worked out with. He said he had found the perfect home for me. It was a place where Hemingway would have been happy. Jay was so excited and he was talking fast. It was a duplex, he said; the upstairs was for rent. It had a high wood-beam ceiling, wood paneling on the walls, large cabinets for storage, a perfect-sized and updated kitchen, a bedroom with a fireplace, and a den. It was near the ocean, where I would feel the cool, healing sea breezes flowing through the rooms and hear the soothing sounds of the surf, and the rooms were full of light. He convinced Raylene, his wife and my friend, to take me to see it.

The house, painted a light sunny yellow, had a white picket fence in front and tall queen palm trees, blue lilies of the Nile, bright orange birds of paradise, and red and green crotons.

I immediately fell in love with the home, and thought that the landlord, Shirley, a dancer, was wonderful. She was warm and kind.

Raylene and I followed her to the upstairs. There were two large windows and I could see the rooftops of the neighbors' homes. I imagined my desk in the large front room. I could write there in the sunlight. I could walk to the beach to take breaks, and Raylene and Jay lived nearby.

I whispered to Raylene, "This is the perfect place for me."

"It is," she encouraged.

But I wasn't sure if Shirley wanted me for a tenant. She seemed tentative and only asked me a few questions. I was trying to seem happy, but I was tired and frightened. It was such a big change, and I wasn't sure if I would be able to climb the fourteen steps from the first to the second floor. I would have to climb the steps slowly so I wouldn't stress my heart, but what would I do if I couldn't climb them at all?

And there were five large potted flowering plants on the patio. They were beautiful, but I didn't want to take care of them. I was so tired of taking care of things and I wondered how I would water them. When I filled the watering can, it would be too heavy for me to lift. I guessed I would have to water them one glassful at a time.

Shirley asked me where I went to high school and I told her in Los Alamitos. She asked me if I'd had a teacher named Erin Spruston, and I said that Mrs. Spruston was my English teacher and inspired me to become a writer. Shirley smiled and said they had been best friends for more than forty years, and I felt like I was in the place I was supposed to be. I had a new home that was only a few steps to the bay, and I was eager to walk to the beach and start swimming.

The following evening, Laura and Charlie invited me over for dinner and I asked them if they thought I could swim in the ocean. Laura glanced at Charlie and asked me if I had spoken with Dr. Rawal. I said I hadn't; I wanted to run the idea by them first.

Charlie looked uncomfortable and said he thought it was too dangerous because the medications I was taking might cause me to pass out in the water.

"Too dangerous to swim for now or forever?" I asked. I couldn't imagine living and not swimming.

"Maybe you will in the future, but you need to check with Dr. Rawal," he advised.

I didn't want to talk with Dr. Rawal and have him reinforce my limitations. I didn't like this part of life.

In the morning, at my workout, when I told Emmy what had happened, I was close to tears, but Emmy bolstered me. She said, "Swimming's in your blood, you will swim again." She was confident.

It was impossible for me to stop thinking about it. I shut down for a few days, but I realized that somehow I needed to get out of my thoughts. Talking with Joe always helped, but I wondered if I was depending on him too much. He had a life, and I kept interrupting it. I just couldn't deal with losing something that was such a big part of me. Maybe, I thought, if I called him, he would tell me a story and get me to think about something else. Maybe that would help. Maybe I could get my mind in a different groove.

I called and asked him to tell me a story about one of his rescues.

He did, and afterward asked, "What's up, buddy?"

"Words have a lot of power. I am not sure I want to talk about it. I'm not sure I want to give these thoughts power," I said.

"You're right, words have power. They affect everything you think and do," he said.

"Or can't do," I said.

"What is it that you can't do?" he asked.

I couldn't speak, and I admonished myself: I should be happy to be alive, have friends and a new home. I should be happy. I am so lucky. But what is life if you can't do the things you love? What's the point? What's the point of all of it? Why did this have to happen to me? Why can't I have a life now? Why can't I just be healthy? Why can't it be my turn? I was so spoiled.

"I'm sorry for bothering you. Everything will be okay."

"Come on, tell me what's happening," he said.

I was afraid if I told him I would start crying and that would be embarrassing.

"You can tell me," he said.

I took a deep breath and said what I needed to fast so I could get it out before I lost it. I told him about my conversation with Charlie. I didn't know if I would ever swim again, and I didn't know if I would get better.

Joe said my body would adjust to the medications, my health would improve, and I would be able to swim again. He was certain. I needed to continue working on my inner dialogue and stop the negative conversations with myself. I needed to meditate and clear my mind. It worked for him. It helped him recover. He was sure it would help me.

"How were you injured?" I asked.

"I fell from a high place and hit hard. I don't want to talk about it," he said.

"Thank God you were okay, Joe," I said.

"Do you believe in God?" he asked, surprised.

"Yes, I do. I never could have done the things I've done without believing in God," I said.

"Okay, before you go to sleep, you need to pray, and before you get out of bed in the morning, you need to pray," he said.

It sounded like a good idea, but I was already meditating two hours a day, and this would take more time.

"What's more important than getting well?" he asked.

Suddenly I understood what this was about. This was like a channel swim but was much bigger. When you do a channel swim, you are pushed off course by the tides and currents, pummeled by fierce wind and waves, and chilled to your bones by the frigid sea, but you keep swimming because something inside yourself says you can push further. You reach deeper within yourself. You swim to see how far you can reach and you swim to see what you will discover within yourself. Something drives you on. Sometimes it's because you believe you can make it. Sometimes it's an awareness that you have to overcome demons of doubt and despair and find courage. Sometimes it's because people don't believe in you and you want to prove your capability to them and yourself. Sometimes you want to do it because people believed you could.

Your tenacity helps determine whether or not you succeed, but it's the ocean that decides if you will reach shore or not. There are channel swims that take you deep, that transform you and make you realize that you are stronger and more tenacious than you ever imagined. You continue swimming simply because you believe you can. You aren't sure. But if you knew you could make it, what would the challenge be? What would you learn? It's working with and against the forces of nature and yourself that transforms you. Each time you do something difficult, you find you can do some more. You change. Your capability increases.

The channels I swam made me look into my heart and soul. They made me see my strengths and weaknesses. They made me face myself. Few things in life compare with this experience. When I finish a channel swim, I know myself well, and that awareness carries into the rest of my life, and through my life. I know it in my heart and soul.

This was the biggest swim of my life. To survive, I needed to take everything I'd learned as an athlete and apply it to overcome these new challenges. It was an epiphany for me. I needed to clearly define my goals, restore my heart function, and live a healthier life. I needed to work with the small crew of trusted experts and close friends who were already guiding me across this channel and cheering me on. I needed to be open to their ideas and committed, consistent, relentless, and spontaneous. I needed to trust my intuition, and when there were moments of serendipity, I needed to realize that there were guiding lights from God leading me along on the right course.

18

DREAMS

It started happening again. When I was fourteen years old I daydreamed about swimming the English Channel. I daydreamed during my classes, in the car, during my workout, when I was in bed. I imagined what it would feel like to swim across the Channel, what it would feel like to climb onto the rocks on the French shore, and how it would feel to break the world record.

The more details people told me about the swim, the more I added to my daydreams. I imagined standing on Shakespeare Beach with the White Cliffs of Dover behind me, the bluebirds flying overhead. In my mind, I heard the surf breaking onto shore and rolling the pebbles on the beach. I imagined the calls of the seagulls, a distant train whistle, and the cool misty air on my skin. I imagined hearing my crew's voices guiding me toward Cap Gris Nez, and the sounds of the escort boat's engine.

Now I started daydreaming about my heart. I imagined my swollen heart beating inside my chest and imagined the ventricle shrinking to normal size. I imagined it was beating slower, the contractions were more forceful, and my heartbeat was more evenly paced.

I imagined the blood flowing through my lungs and the oxygen binding to the hemoglobin in my blood, releasing energy and healing my heart muscle.

It had been a long time since I remembered my dreams, but I started having a recurring dream about my heart. The only time I had had a recurring dream before was when I was waiting to swim around the Cape of Good Hope. There was a large great white shark population in the area. I planned to have policemen from Cape Town, who were trained like a special forces team, in the water with me to watch for sharks. But I was concerned that my support crew might not see a great white in time to warn me.

I had a dream that during the swim I was chased by a great white shark and sprinted to the support boat. The crew managed to pull me out of the water before I was bitten. The dream helped me prepare for the shark—a twelve-foot-long aggressive bronze whaler shark—that came up for me during the swim. I swam closer to the support boat, and trusted my sharpshooter in the water to deter the shark and enable me to complete the swim.

The recurring dream I was having about my heart was so vivid that when I awoke, it seemed real.

In the dream I felt something crawling across my chest. When I looked down I saw a large hole in my chest above my heart. I could see my heart beating. It was dark red, normally shaped, but there were white worms half as long as my little finger inching their way out of my heart. They were climbing out of the hole and crawling away across my chest. My subconscious was working while I was sleeping and ridding my heart of negative parasites. They were leaving my body and my heart was growing lighter because it wasn't carrying the weight of the parasites.

I told Joe about the dream and how helpful it was to imagine negative thoughts as parasites, and how by making those thoughts into creatures inside my body, it motivated me to purge them. I said I was feeling better in every way. But I was sad because I missed my mom.

"Why are you provoking grief?" he asked.

Provoking grief? I said to myself. Was I doing that? Why was I stirring up feelings of sadness and loss? Why would I want to bring up those painful feelings? I didn't need to relive those sad things. Why would I provoke grief when I was doing well? Being sad was a feeling I had endured for a long time. I didn't enjoy it, but it was something I knew well. I was comfortable with the internal script that went with being sad. I didn't know what else to expect and feel. But I was undoing my progress by provoking grief. I had a choice. I didn't need to provoke grief. I could choose to be happy. It was a big realization for me.

The day I learned I might lose my heart, I started talking to it, and the conversation has never stopped. This helped me stay connected with what I was feeling emotionally and physically, and it helped make me aware of how my heart was responding.

Each day I told my heart that I was happy that she was still a part of me, and I was grateful for her. I told her that she was strong and powerful and that she would endure like she always had. I told my heart that I loved her, that I always wanted her with me. We still had great things we would do together, and I wanted to do them wholeheartedly.

19

SYNCHRONICITY

Ed Schlenk, the doctor from Iowa, and I spoke once in a while on the phone. He said I had experienced a lot of emotional loss and grief and might have things I needed to work through. It might help me to speak with a psychologist.

I was feeling okay but was willing to speak to a professional if that would help my recovery.

The same day, Bob Swoap e-mailed me. Bob was a clinical psychologist and psychology professor at Warren Wilson College in North Carolina. He was an acquaintance of Oliver Sacks.

Oliver was my swimming buddy and one of the world's most famous neurologists and psychiatrists. Oliver was a professor of neurology and psychiatry at Columbia University Medical Center, a professor at the NYU School of Medicine, and a best-selling author. He wrote about his patients' neurological afflictions with incredible insight and compassion and he focused on the magnificent adaptations they made to live their lives as fully as possible. He also wrote about his own health challenges and explained how he overcame them.

Oliver had initially put Bob Swoap in touch with me. Bob was a sports psychologist who was writing an article for *Blue Ridge Outdoors* magazine. He asked if he could interview me about my mind-set during my open-water swims, how I overcame uncertainties and fear, and how I kept working toward my goal when I was discouraged. He believed this information would help other people achieve their goals.

We talked on the phone for a long time. His questions were thoughtful and different because he understood the mental challenges people faced when they were working toward their goals.

The interview became uncomfortable when he asked if I was still swimming. I didn't want to talk about not being able to swim so I told him I was busy with my new book and was only working out in the gym, but I hoped to get back into the water sometime.

He asked if I was going on a book tour soon. He said he had heard book tours could be exhausting. It was funny; he seemed to ask all the questions I didn't want to answer. I wasn't sure if I was going to be strong enough to go on the book tour, if my heart could handle the stress, and I was afraid of having a setback, but I didn't want to discuss this with him either.

I said I was working on coordinating the tour with my publisher and planning to build in rests along the way so I could pace myself like I did on a long swim.

Bob said he had been a swimmer since childhood, but open-water swimming was new to him. He had recently competed in an open-water swim and was hoping to do more in the future. His coach was planning to compete in a lake swim in northern Vermont and wanted advice on cold-water conditioning and navigation. We talked about how he and his coach could train.

Bob asked if I was training for a big swim, and I thought to myself, He seems to be touching on everything that I'm dealing with. I said I was working on being healthy.

He asked if he could call back in a few days with follow-up questions. He had a positive attitude, was insightful, and was good at building rapport. I looked forward to talking with him again.

When he phoned I answered his questions and told him I thought it was synchronicity that he had contacted me the day Ed suggested I speak with a psychologist. I asked him if it would be okay to talk with him about something personal. He said he would be happy to help if he could.

I summarized what had happened with my life and heart, and explained ejection fractions.

Bob already knew all about ejection fractions. He had worked and conducted research at Duke University Medical Center as a health psychologist. Patients who were at risk for or who had had cardiac arrests worked with him to change their behaviors to reduce their chances of having heart attacks. He used cognitive-behavioral techniques to help them make changes. These included stress management, eating better, becoming more active, and developing deeper connections with friends and family.

It seemed amazing that Bob had gotten in touch with me. As a sports psychologist he understood athletes, having worked with them from the recreational to the Olympic level. And as a health psychologist, Bob understood the effects of the mind on the heart and vice versa.

"I'm not sure I heard what you said. What did you say your EF is?" Bob asked. He sounded incredulous.

"It was fifteen," I said.

"That *is* low, but you said you are feeling better?"

"Yes, I'm a lot better," I said and told him the changes I had made in my life: improving my diet, reducing my calorie intake, gradually increasing my exercise, hanging out with positive friends, praying and meditating, and trying to let go of negative thoughts, changing my internal dialogue, and being aware of things that were stressing me so I could figure out how to deal with them or get myself out of stressful situations.

Bob said I was making changes that would help me and I was doing well. He offered to talk again if I got stuck. He was reassuring, and I was glad we had talked. I felt like I was doing better with my mental focus, but I was still searching for ways to help my heart function improve.

20

HEART CELLS

"There's something that we've been missing," Joe the fireman said.

For two months he had been trying to figure out why I had become ill. He thought it was caused by something more than the stress of life. Had my daily routine changed?

I didn't think so.

He asked me the last time I'd done a long-distance cold-water swim.

It had been five years.

He asked me the last time I had consistently trained in the ocean.

It had been more than two years.

That was what we had been missing. My heart had been acclimated to cold, and I had suddenly stopped swimming in cold water. The cold stimulus had been removed and that had affected me negatively. He thought I needed to get back into the cold to get well.

He made sense to me. I remembered when, after my first English Channel swim, my dad phoned me in Dover and asked me how I was feeling. I was tired and elated. At age fifteen I had become the youngest and fastest person to swim the English Channel, but my neck and shoulders were sore from lifting my head too many times to see the French coast. I also had intense muscle cramps in my calves when I went to bed, and the muscles between my ribs ached. He explained that the intercostal muscles, the muscles between my ribs, were used to support my breathing. I had worked and breathed hard for almost ten hours and I had stressed the muscles. The cramps in my legs could have been caused by muscle fatigue or dehydration or an electrolyte imbalance. I needed to rehydrate and eat bananas and oranges to rebalance my electrolytes. Most important, I needed to detrain, which would help take the soreness out of my body, allow me to stretch and relax, and allow my body to adjust to a lighter workout.

Detraining was a concept that I had not heard of. My dad explained that I had trained hard for years to swim the English Channel. It would be too much of a shock to my body and mind to suddenly stop working out. I had to detrain—gradually reduce my time in the water. That morning I needed to swim in Dover Harbor for two hours, the next day I would swim for at least an hour and a half, and when I arrived home I planned to continue tapering my workouts. Then I could take time off, but my body was accustomed to being active, so I needed to continue walking, lifting weights, and doing calisthenics and other activities.

If I detrained, my body would have a chance to acclimate to the reduced workload. Hearts and bodies do not adapt well to sudden changes.

My dad also explained that I had worked hard and long to achieve a big goal and it would be a big psychological letdown if I just stopped swimming. He said I needed to give my mind a chance to adjust too.

After I swam the English Channel, the last thing I wanted to do was to go for a swim the following morning. I wanted to relax and enjoy the success with my mom and friends. But my dad knew things about the mind and body.

Joe knew a lot about training too and I agreed that I needed to get back in cold water—but I couldn't swim.

He laughed and said I didn't have to go swimming to be in cold water. I needed to reintroduce my heart cells to the cold. He suggested that I hold a cold wet dish towel for at least five minutes each day and measure the water temperature, my blood pressure, and my heart rate both before and after.

He said that it might sound like a strange thing to do, but he thought it would help.

It didn't sound strange to me. It sounded like a fantastic idea. Joe didn't know about all the experiments Dr. Keatinge had conducted on me at the University of London. He didn't know that my response to the cold was dramatic, and that it was different from other test subjects'. But I had not been training in the cold and so I had lost my acclimatization.

"Joe, could I reacclimatize faster if I put my hand in cold water?" I asked. I was excited about testing his idea.

"You need to reintroduce your heart to the cold gradually. You need to give yourself time. Don't sabotage yourself," he warned.

"What do you mean?" I asked.

"People try to do too much too soon, and they get hurt. That causes a setback and slows down their healing process. You need to build back gradually. Be smart. Start by holding the cold wet towel."

I was excited to test Joe's idea. I measured my blood pressure. It was 111/73 and my heart rate was 58 beats per minute. I submerged a dish towel in 57 degree Fahrenheit water (13.9 degrees centigrade), squeezed out the excess, and held the towel over the sink.

It was good to be in touch with the cool water again. It felt like I was holding on to a piece of home. I smiled and relaxed. When five minutes had passed, I set the cloth down and measured my blood pressure. It was 113/62 and my heart rate had increased to 97 beats per minute.

My heart rate had significantly increased after I held on to the cold cloth. It could have been because I had an irregular heartbeat, but when I sequentially measured my heart rate, I didn't see this much difference. When

I walked into the ocean, my heart rate and breathing increased until my body adjusted to the cold water. When I started swimming my heart rate and breathing slowed down. My response to the cold towel was the same as my response to walking into the cold ocean. It was exciting.

21

MOVED

The day after Valentine's Day my friends helped me pack my things and loaded them into their cars. I followed them out of the neighborhood and felt sad and happy— sad for the home and friends I was leaving and happy for my new home and the friends I would make. I remembered an encouraging line from Tennyson: *The shell must break before the bird can fly.*

It was time to fly.

Raylene, Jay, and Emmy carried boxes and plastic bags up the fourteen steps to my new home. The place was perfect, but I was concerned. I had to climb the steps slowly so I wouldn't overstress my heart. What would happen if my health suddenly declined and I couldn't climb the steps? I wanted to believe that I would recover.

I couldn't lift or carry much, and my friends wouldn't let me carry anything. They asked me to direct them and let them know where I wanted them to put my things.

Kathleen Fessenden and Lorraine Afzali, longtime

friends, arrived, and they organized my clothes in the closet, my books in the bookcase, and my mementos on some shelves.

In less than three hours they had moved me in.

When I left my old home, I took my clothes and bed and not much else, and my friends knew that I would need many things in my home. Cindy Palin and Sandy Field unpacked a week's worth of food and put it in the refrigerator and the pantry. I ordered some pizza. More friends arrived. We opened some bottles of wine and used my new wineglasses to toast my new home, health, and good friends. All I thought was how lucky I am to be loved and have great friends.

22

APRIL 5—ELATED

On April 5, I was scheduled to have a follow-up echocardiogram. Laura King asked if she could accompany me. She wanted to discuss the test results with Dr. Rawal. She didn't want to have us wait a month for the test results. If Dr. Rawal wasn't in the office for the test, she would talk with her friends, Dr. Isaac Eisenstein and Dr. William Madrid, and ask them to take a look at the echocardiogram.

Laura was determined to hear the results.

I didn't understand why the echocardiogram was that important.

We drove over together and she phoned the office manager to make sure that a doctor would be in the office to read the echo. The office manager said the test was scheduled during lunchtime and she wasn't sure if a doctor would be in to read it.

Laura said we would wait for one.

Laura sat in the waiting area while I went into the

exam room. But a few minutes later, she tried to convince the tech to let her watch him do the echo.

He said it was against policy and told me that in the fifteen years he had worked as an echocardiogram tech, he had never had anyone try to convince him to let them come in to observe the exam. He said that she must be a close friend.

I said she was, and I heard her voice in the hallway.

The door opened and a tall, strong, middle-aged man with brown eyes, brown hair, and a big smile walked into the room. He said his name was Dr. Madrid. He was a good friend of Laura's. She wanted him to take a look at the echocardiogram. Would I be okay if he did?

"That would be great," I said.

He looked at the screen.

"It looks like her ejection fraction is forty-five!" he exclaimed. "She may be back in normal sinus rhythm!"

He instructed the echocardiogram tech, "When you finish, ask Judy to do an electrocardiogram, an EKG!" He sounded excited.

He left to see another patient, but he stopped to give Laura the results.

"That's excellent news!" she said.

Judy led me into the EKG room, ran the test, and handed the EKG paper to Dr. Madrid.

He put his hand on my shoulder while he looked at the EKG. He said my ejection fraction was fifty. My heart wasn't back in normal sinus rhythm, but it was moving in the right direction. I asked him what he meant.

He said my heart was mechanically functioning in a way that was close to normal sinus rhythm. He was so excited.

"Look, your heart rate was one hundred fifty-seven beats per minute and it was in arrhythmia when you were here in December. Look at it now four months later. It's down to seventy-four beats per minute!"

Dr. Rawal entered the hallway and looked as if he wondered what all the commotion was about. The women at the front desk were smiling, his partner was smiling. Dr. Madrid told him to take a look at the echocardiogram and the EKG.

Dr. Rawal put his arm around my shoulder. He was beaming.

"This is great news!" he said.

It was the first time I had seen him so excited and happy.

"You can start exercising more. You can increase your intensity. You need to start swimming again, but make sure to swim with a buddy."

I was thrilled. I was a lot better and I could swim again.

He said I would need to continue taking the heart medications, but I had made a fantastic improvement.

I was excited about being able to swim in the ocean, but I knew I wasn't ready. I needed to gradually get my body used to the cold water. And I was scared. Before I was sick, I was lifting twenty-pound free weights in every workout; now I could only lift five pounds. I had lost so much muscle strength, and my arms were flabby where my muscles had been. And I had lost endurance. I wondered if I could swim fifty meters and I was afraid. I knew this was contrary to what Dr. Rawal was telling me. He had said it was okay for me to swim, but my body wasn't as strong as it had once been, and I was on medications that were helping my heart function normally, but I didn't know how they would affect me when I swam in cold water. The medications helped my heart to relax and pump more efficiently, but they caused my blood vessels to dilate. I was concerned. I had trained for years to constrict my blood vessels when I swam in cold water so I could keep my core temperature normal. By dilating my blood vessels with the medication, I would lose body heat to the water. I didn't know if I would be able to keep my core temperature normal, and if I couldn't, I wondered how much stress that would place on my heart. I didn't know how my body would respond to the cold. I didn't know if Dr. Rawal would understand this because I knew my body was different. It had allowed me to do extraordinary swims.

On the drive home, Laura was grinning. She said there was something she hadn't told me because she didn't want me to worry. She said this had been a big day for me. The results of the echo had been important. If my heart hadn't shown an improvement, I would have needed a pacemaker and defibrillator, and I would have been put on the heart transplant list.

She hadn't wanted to wait for the results because she

couldn't wait that long. She and Charlie thought I was getting better, but they were nervous about the results of the echo.

Now they thought my recovery would be complete.

The result confirmed for me that the things I was doing were helping me get better. I was thrilled, but I wanted to figure out what more I could do to recover more quickly.

23

APRIL KISSES

The sun was veiled by a thin layer of cloud, but the sky was bright gray, and tree branches were covered in red and green buds. I walked through Central Park past small gardens filled with yellow, white, and orange daffodils and grape hyacinths.

Earth's energy surged around me. I don't remember spring ever being as beautiful. A flock of sparrows were singing in the trees, robins were pulling worms from vibrant green lawns, and blue jays were feasting on acorns. The earth smelled sweet.

People were walking through the park smiling, riding bikes, jogging, pushing strollers, and walking their dogs. They felt the new energy of spring.

Walking out of Central Park, around Columbus Circle, and onto Broadway, I felt the wind funneling between high buildings. It was blowing from the Hudson River and tiny snowflakes were moving in swirling waves, making the variation in the wind's speed and direction visible.

The clouds parted, and the sun burst through. Sunlight warmed the city and the snowflakes disappeared.

I walked down Broadway, past Times Square, with giant neon signs aglow, to the West Village. Oliver Sacks was waiting to see me. He was celebrating his eightieth birthday and I couldn't wait to give him some Baci, the Italian dark chocolates filled with a hazelnut center. *Baci* translated to English means "kisses." Each kiss had a message about love written on a small piece of paper. The message was written in Italian, French, German, and English.

Oliver loved chocolate and it surprised me that he had never tasted Baci. I opened one for him, and he popped it in his mouth and savored the creamy chocolate and crunchy hazelnut. I straightened out the message written on the paper and read it to him. It was a saying about the heart and endurance. He liked the message. I asked him if he wanted another so I could read him another message. He grinned and his brown eyes lit up.

The message was about love, and I thought about how much I loved him and that we had been friends for a long time. I remembered the first time we met. I had read an article about him in a swimming magazine. I had read his books, but I didn't know that he was a swimmer. His father, a physician, started teaching him to swim when he was just a week old. From that moment, he loved being in the water. As an adolescent, he swam with his family in the sea off the coast of England, and as an adult

he swam in pools and oceans. He wrote about interesting people, many of whom were born with or acquired
different afflictions, and he wrote about the lessons he
learned from them. He seemed to have an insatiable curi-
osity about life. I was intrigued by him and wanted to
meet him so I called his office and left a voice message. I
told him that I had read an article about him and that I
was coming to New York City to try to get my first book
published.

Oliver returned my call five minutes later and said that
he had been following my career for years. He wanted to
know if we could go for a swim, and to know more about
the book I wanted to get published. He thought he might
be able to help.

We met at his office in Greenwich Village. He drove
his sporty white Lexus through Manhattan to the swimming pool with the agility and anticipation of a race car
driver. I commented on how well he drove and he smiled
and said that he used to ride a motorcycle. It helped him
hone his response time. He said that when he was working on a graduate degree at UCLA he rode his motorcycle
on Mulholland Drive. He rode it a number of times, then
decided to close his eyes and see if he could ride sections
of it from memory. I didn't think that was a good idea,
but I liked the way he tested himself. He mentioned that
he was also a champion weight lifter. He could bench-
press nearly five hundred pounds.

We shared a lane in the swimming pool. He swam backstroke and some breaststroke, but he loved backstroke, and his stroke was smooth, and strong, and beautiful. We watched each other swim and he admired my backstroke and asked if I had any suggestions. I told him to press his back into the water so his hips would lift and to bend his elbow more on the underwater pull, so that he would push more water. He was in tune with his body and its movement through the water and made an immediate change that let him swim faster.

When we finished working out and climbed out of the pool, he wrote notes on a waterproof tablet with an erasable pen. I asked what he was doing. He said he got ideas about work, writing, and his patients while he was swimming and he wrote them down so he wouldn't forget. I said I got some of my best ideas when I was swimming. He smiled and said that swimming was a time when we could meditate.

When we returned to his office, Oliver invited me to have lunch with Michael, one of his patients. Michael had one of the most dramatic cases of Tourette's syndrome Oliver had ever seen. He explained that Tourette's was a neuropsychiatric disorder. Michael had physical and vocal tics. He made inappropriate and derogatory remarks and used offensive language. He couldn't control these tics. If he tried, they only grew worse. Oliver wanted to make sure I felt comfortable having lunch with Michael. I felt honored that Oliver wanted to bring me into his world.

We met Michael and walked across the street from Oliver's office to a British restaurant and sat down at a table. Michael turned to a man sitting at a table beside ours and said that he was sorry, but he had Tourette's and that he might slap or punch him or say something inappropriate. The man nodded that he understood.

Oliver sat across from us, and we ordered lunch. Michael slapped me on the leg and called me inappropriate names. I made a joke of what he had said, and we laughed. Oliver said that Michael was a swimmer too. He discovered that if people who had Tourette's did repetitive motions, they became calmer and had fewer outbursts. Swimming and gardening at the New York Botanical Garden helped Michael relax. So we talked about swimming and gardening, things I loved to do too. After we finished lunch and Michael left, Oliver said he was surprised that I was so at ease with Michael. I said it had to be difficult to live Michael's life, not to be able to control his body movements and to say things he didn't intend. Michael seemed like he had a good heart.

Oliver nodded.

After that lunch Oliver asked me to stay in touch with him and said he would help me in any way he could with my first book. Through the years we wrote to each other, and he introduced me to his friends and colleagues and we discussed their work and passions. When I flew to New York City, we swam and had a meal with friends and discussed the topics we were writing about, and when he traveled to California for a conference we met to do the same. We talked about his lectures, octopuses and cuttlefish, Auden's poetry, neurological disorders, nature, Mexico, and our travels and discoveries.

Oliver exposed me to worlds I would never have experienced.

Now, many years later, he was sitting with his back to the window in a halo of light. He had his hands clasped behind his head. He said the ginkgo trees were leafing; they were one of his favorite trees because they could endure the extreme cold of New York City in winter and survive the heat of summer. He was happy it was finally spring.

I wondered if he felt the increased oxygen in the air with the leafing of the trees and increased photosynthesis. I wondered if I should tell him that I was ill. He was one of my closest friends. I loved him, and I didn't want to make him sad or worried about me.

I asked him how he was.

He said he was doing well but had lost vision in one eye to cancer, and he was almost blind in the other eye. It was challenging for him to see what he wrote, until he figured out how to enlarge the print and hold a magnifying glass above the page. It took both for him to read text. He was still swimming and hoped that next time we met, we could swim together.

He asked me how my mom was doing.

I told him she had passed away.

He suddenly looked sad and said it was difficult to lose a parent.

He asked me how I was doing. I decided to tell him that I had been sick, and my doctor friends thought I had broken heart syndrome.

As he listened to my story about what had happened, he looked sad and serious, but when I finished talking, he said that he knew I would recover fully. He understood how the heart and mind worked together, and he knew mine were very strong.

"Oliver, maybe someday you will write about my broken heart," I said softly.

"Maybe someday you will," he said, and smiled.

He changed the subject and said he was working on an article about being tickled, and he asked me if I remembered being tickled, or tickling someone, and if I liked being tickled.

I told him I was ticklish and shared some of my memories.

He smiled and stored the stories somewhere in his mind.

"You know you can't tickle yourself," he said.

"Never thought of that," I said and tried to tickle my arm. He was right.

He glanced at his watch. I had to go and catch a flight but told him that the next time we met, we could go swimming.

A couple of days later Oliver wrote and said that he

was sorry to hear about my mother's death, all the stress that had occurred around it, and its effect on me. He was sure I would regain my strength and health, that nothing was as good for me as writing. I hoped I could be as brave as he was.

24

THE SINK

I put the black rubber stopper in the deep white kitchen sink and opened the faucet. The sound of the water reminded me of Song, my bright yellow canary. He loved to sing when I turned on the water, he loved to sing with the water's song. He tweeted and trilled. His song was bright like the sound of rolling water. When I turned the faucet and increased the water flow, he sang his aria louder and hit higher notes. Happiness flowed from him, and his song filled the house.

As he sang I would walk outside to the garden, snap tops off the basil plants, ones that were flowering and going to seed, and use a clothespin to hold them inside Song's cage.

When he smelled the basil, he leapt from rung to rung in the cage, pulled the soft white seeds from the tops, and crushed them in his beak. He ate for a few moments, then stopped, looked at me with his tiny dark eyes, and sang a song of thanks.

When I returned to the sink, he sang with all his heart. The air was perfumed with sweet basil. I closed my eyes and listened to Song sing with the water.

Now I placed my hands under the faucet, and the shimmering water splashed off my hands. It felt so good, but it was too warm. I needed to acclimate to cooler water to be able to swim in the ocean. Joe suggested adding ice cubes.

Reaching into the freezer, I grabbed three handfuls of ice cubes and dunked my hands under the water. The ice floated to the surface and left a melting chill. I opened my hands, stretched them, and let them float with the ice cubes. The cold made me feel alive, and it stirred something deep within me.

I moved my hands back and forth in a sculling motion. I sculled stronger and faster and watched my hand motions create bubbles. My heart beat faster, and I smiled, moved my hands faster, and felt my breathing increase. It felt so good to be in the cold water again. It felt like it was about 56 degrees Fahrenheit (13.3 degrees centigrade). I measured it with a pool thermometer. It was the same as the ocean. Perfect.

I pulled the water toward me and reached out farther in front of me. My muscles remembered the feeling. I watched the water move and bounce off the sides of the sink. I listened to the sounds of the water change as I increased my speed.

My body was moving with the flow of the water. I was dog-paddling. My head was high out of the water. My hands were below my chest. I was pulling and churning the water.

My heart was beating more evenly in my chest and my breaths were deep and relaxed.

Leaning forward, I extended my arms until my knuckles touched the far side of the sink and lengthened my pulls. My hands were moving from one side of the sink to the other. I took a deep breath and began counting: one two three, one two three. I was exhaling as I was counting. I didn't realize I was turning my head to one side to take a breath, exhaling facedown toward the sink, and turning my head to the other side to take a breath. It was all happening automatically. I kept moving my arms and increased my stroke motion. I popped my elbow up, and reached to the far side of the sink, put my hand in the water, took three strokes, exhaled, turned my head to breathe, inhaled, turned my face back to the sink, and counted three more strokes. I closed my eyes. I forgot where I was. I felt my body rotating, my arms pulling, heard the sound of my breath, and felt the water moving. It felt wonderful.

I laughed at myself. I once swam the English Channel and now was swimming in the sink. I had fallen so far, but I was trying to find my way back.

I played with my pulls, pulled fast and slow, pulled deep and shallow, watched my hands move and let them float on the water. It was crazy to swim in the sink, but it had been a long time since I'd had so much fun.

In the evening, I found my yellow swim cap and tinted goggles packed away in a closet. I filled the sink with water, added ice. My cap still smelled like the sea, and when I licked my goggles to clear them and keep them from fogging, I tasted salt.

Again, I swam in the sink, I closed my eyes, and in my mind, I was back in the ocean, diving beneath the surf, swimming across the surface of the shimmering sea. I was listening to the breath of the wind and waves, the call of the seagulls, the music of the fog horn, the rumble of boat engines. I was swimming along the buoy line, watching the sailboats glide by, the kite surfers skimming across the water's surface at breathtaking speeds. I was feeling strong, balanced in the water, my arm strokes were long and powerful, my heart was beating evenly, and my breaths were deep and easy.

Soon I would be in the ocean again. I knew it in my heart.

25

MAY 7—NOT YET

I continued my daily swims in the sink and did all the other things I had been doing to get well.

Dr. Rawal met with me in the examination room. It was May and I was feeling stronger. He listened to my heart and lungs and said, "You're doing fantastic. I don't want you to have any restrictions, and I don't think you should place any restrictions on yourself. Have you started swimming again?"

"I haven't," I said.

"I think you need to start swimming again. Your ejection fraction was fifteen, and now you're at fifty. You're at a low normal," he said.

Low normal is good, I thought, but it's not sixty.

"You said I don't need to put any limits on myself. How far can I swim?" I asked.

"I don't think you should swim the Catalina Channel." He paused and said under his breath, "Not yet."

I smiled to myself. He didn't know that was a trigger for me. When I tried to swim the Bering Strait, the Soviets told me *"nyet."* *Nyet* means no, but I translated the word to mean "not yet."

Not yet was good. I didn't have any desire to swim the Catalina Channel. I had completed it twice, and I had broken all records for that swim. I didn't need to repeat it. I told Dr. Rawal about Joe and the way I was reacclimating to the water, and of my concerns about overstimulating the vagus nerve by getting into cold water too fast and having that put stress on my heart. I explained that I was reintroducing my body very gradually to colder water so I could adapt gradually. Dr. Rawal listened intently; he agreed with what I was doing and advised me to continue working out in the gym and to keep my heart rate below 110.

He was thrilled with my progress. His reactions were so different from when I first started seeing him when he had been not at all optimistic.

I felt another hurdle had been cleared, an enormous achievement, but my goal was to have a normal ejection fraction and get off the medications. I needed to figure out what else I could do. I found inspiration in reconnecting with the Simonelli family. My fourth book had been published, and Liana's mom dropped her off at my book signing in Del Mar, California. Pearl, her younger sister, wanted to join us, but she was at a swim meet. Liana was an avid reader and was enthralled by the book writing process. We talked about the book signing after lunch at a nearby restaurant, and we discussed her swimming goals and school. She was thirteen years old, training hard for Junior Olympics, and studying many hours a day to gain admittance to a top-notch high school. She said she was doing very well and asked me how I was doing. I said that I had been very sick, but I was a lot better, partly due to the time I spent with her and her family. I told her I loved being with them, that they were a kind and loving family, and that I had learned that love could help me heal my heart. She nodded slowly like an adult. She said she knew something had been wrong with me, and she was very happy I was better. She asked me if I was swimming, and I told her I was, but that it had been a strange way back. I felt foolish, but I said, "I started back by swimming in the sink."

She said, "That's so beautiful. You are taking baby steps to swim again and recover."

I nodded and thought, She knows so much for being so young. I told her I was thinking about using swimming in the sink as the title for my new book.

Liana smiled and her brown eyes filled with light. "I love that title. You know, when my parents taught me and Pearl how to swim, they taught us in the sink. The tub was too big for us."

"I learned in the tub and had to revert to the sink," I said, and we laughed.

I was starting over at a smaller place than where I began, just like training for a channel swim. I had to think, train, learn from experts, piece the information together, and use it to help me succeed. But there was something holding me back.

26

JULY 2—FLOATING

I stepped into Alamitos Bay, off the shores of Long Beach, California, and felt the cool salt water flow over my feet and up to my ankles, and the chill traveled through my blood to my heart. I was back in the water. I smiled and inhaled fast. This was my breakthrough. Even though the water only reached my ankles, I realized that I was on the path that would give me confidence and help me transform my life. The strength in my heart was returning and I felt ready to embrace life again.

Each day I walked in the water along the edge of the bay. Tiny waves rushed over my feet and tugged me toward the sea. I felt more peaceful than before, and stronger. I gazed across the bright blue beveled water and up at the bright blue sky. I studied the line where the two met and thought the same thing I had dreamed about as a child: Maybe someday I will swim to the horizon.

But before I could swim I needed to walk. For an hour each day I walked along the edge of the bay to acclimate to the cold water, and by June I was walking in knee-deep water the length of the shore. The shock of the cold diminished. My heart was beating stronger, and I was happier than I had been for years.

Every day I walked, I had the chance to jump in the water and swim, but something was holding me back.

Martha Kaplan invited me to spend the Fourth of July weekend in the country with her, Vicky, Andy, Kathy, and other friends from Knopf. It sounded like it would be a fun and fascinating weekend. The Knopf family always had intriguing discussions, and I was so happy to be part of that group. Martha told me I could swim in Andy's new pond. It sounded like a good idea, but I was reluctant.

Joe once told me that before he went into a burning building, he planned his exit, and he made sure he had multiple exits. The pond was in the country where cell phones didn't work. If I had a problem in the water, Martha wasn't strong enough to pull me out, and she didn't know CPR. It would take fifteen minutes or more for the first responders to reach the pond. I wasn't sure if I wanted to get in the water.

We arrived at Martha's place in the late afternoon. The air was hot, heavy, and humid, and our clothes and bugs were biting us. Martha spoke with Andy and said the pond was warm and perfect for a swim.

It was strange: for months I had dreamed about swimming again, but it was much easier to dream about it and work toward it than it was to do it. It was like life—easier to dream about than to do.

I had fallen so far. I was afraid that I might not be able to swim across the pond. I wasn't sure if I wanted to know what I could do. My heart was improving, but I hadn't been swimming, and my body was weak. I was worried that if I got into the pond, I might not be able to climb out.

"Martha, if something happens, you need to know that I'm not your responsibility, okay?" I said.

"You'll be fine," she said in her happy voice.

She didn't know that my arms were weak and flabby. She didn't know how much I had lost.

I changed into my swimsuit and rode with Martha and her dog Frankie to Andy's.

The shrubs around his home that had been bare in December were now covered with lush green foliage. The elegant magnolias and roses were blooming and perfuming the air. And the once-frozen stream was flowing fast. All the air bubbles had been released from the ice and the water was tumbling over rocks. I had been sabotaging myself, limiting myself with doubt.

We climbed the hill in Andy's backyard. Frankie led the way. She held her spotted black-and-white tail high and wagged it. She reminded me of Beth Snow Flower, my Dalmatian, the dog I swam with in my grandparents' pond when I was a child. Snow Pond was where I learned to swim, and I remembered how much I loved it.

The air was sweltering and oppressive. Perspiration was running down my cheeks and the back of my knees. I told myself it would feel so good to get into the water.

Andy's pond was small and perfectly round. I thought, I am coming full circle. It's so strange how life is; you never know where it's going to take you. I was grateful I had the chance to come full circle and had the chance to try to swim again.

It started sprinkling. The sky was pastel shades of gray that were growing darker with the clouds building on the horizon. The wind was increasing, and the clouds were moving toward us.

On a steep hill high above Andy's pond, black-and-white dairy cattle were grazing on tender green grass. In an adjacent field a farmer was riding his red tractor and cutting hay. He increased his speed. If we were going to swim, we needed to do it quickly; it looked like the clouds were thunderheads.

Martha jumped into the pond with Frankie. White water exploded around them like an uncorked bottle of champagne. The sounds of their splashes sounded like fun. I wanted to jump in too, but I sat on a flat rock, dipped my legs in the warm water, and kicked slowly to awaken and stretch my muscles. The warm water pulled the heat from my body and it felt wonderful. I wasn't sure what I would be able to do. I wasn't sure if my arms would support me. I was scared. I was scared of the water. Was I going to be okay?

"Come on in. The water's great," Martha exclaimed

and rolled onto her back, exhaled, and swam backstroke. Ripples of slivery water flowed off her muscular arms, red swimsuit, and long legs. The tiny waves slid to the sides of the pond.

The pond was small and sensitive to the slightest movement. It would only take four or five strokes to swim across. I stopped kicking and let my feet float to the surface. They looked so pale, but they weren't swollen.

I stepped into the water and felt my feet sink deep into the silty bottom. The silt rose up in a cloud around me. The water was hot along the pond's edge, but when I stepped into deeper water, the temperature dropped and took my breath away. The pond was fed by cold artesian springs.

I looked at the sky. The wind was blowing even harder and black clouds were racing toward us.

If you're going to get in, get in now, or you won't have a chance today, I told myself. Remember to get in slowly, give yourself and your heart time to adjust to the water.

I walked in. The water was marbled warm and cold. I lay on my stomach and floated facedown, dropped my ears below the surface so I could listen to the silence. I loved that silence. I loved the way the water smelled so sweet. I turned my head and listened to the water's song, grabbed my knees, and did the jellyfish float like I did as a child. I listed to one side and then the other, adjusted my balance, and found my center. My heart was beating in my ears: it was strong and steady, and everything was okay.

Rolling onto my back, I floated and felt soft raindrops tickle my face. I floated in the space between the earth and sky. My body and spirit felt light.

The rain pattered on my face. I loved being in the water during a storm. The pond was covered with large waves, trees were swaying, creaking, and bending, and leaves were blowing in a wild frenzy.

In the distance, above steep hills, red lightning flashed in the black sky, and thunder rumbled. The wind increased. Dark clouds were moving fast. Tendrils of white lightning lit the sky. Thunder crackled and boomed. I counted the number of seconds between the thunder and lightning. For every five seconds that separated the two, the storm was one mile away. I counted fifty seconds. The heart of the storm was ten miles away, but there was a lot of energy in the storm. It was approaching fast. Black clouds were dropping to earth and the lightning was beginning to glow neon blue.

I had only floated for fifteen minutes, and I wanted to stay in longer, but the lightning was now less than three miles away. I picked up my soggy towel and ran with Martha and Frankie to the car. We jumped in and shut the doors just as lightning struck and lit the hill near the pond.

Frankie panted and wisely crouched in the backseat. The rain fell so fast and heavy that all we saw was water pouring down on the windshield. Overhead the lightning flashed and thunder boomed louder. Nothing rivaled the beauty or power of nature's fireworks. We waited until the storm subsided before Martha drove us home.

The next day Martha, Vicky, and I took a road trip to Binghamton, New York, a city at the confluence of the Susquehanna and Chenango Rivers. We went hunting for antiques, but I wasn't a good shopper. After a few hours, I was ready to do something else, but Vicky and Martha were just starting their day of hunting.

Martha told me, "These are things that someone once loved," and that helped me appreciate the intrinsic value of these objects, but I didn't need a wooden rocking horse, a statue of a giant frog, an ancient bicycle, or dishes. There were old books, and I stopped to slowly flip through their pages.

In the late afternoon we returned to Andy's pond and I couldn't wait to swim. I walked in and leaned forward so my chest touched the water and my arms floated on the surface. I started moving my arms like I was swimming. It was a lot easier swimming standing up in the water than it was swimming in the sink. I extended my arms as far as they could reach, pulled the water with my hands, kept my elbows high as I pulled, rotated my body to the side with each stroke, and pulled the water until I brushed my thumbs against my thighs.

My arms and back felt sore from lack of conditioning. I dipped my face in the water. It woke something inside and I felt my heart beat faster.

It's time. You're ready, I encouraged myself.

I took a deep breath and pushed off the bottom. The cool water lifted and enveloped me and I was free from the weight of the earth and lighthearted. I swam four strokes, turned around, and swam back. I did it again and I felt the energy returning to my body. I swam faster and watched my arms move underwater. They were flabby, as the muscles had atrophied. I had lost a lot of weight and was able to swim easily, but my arms felt weak.

I told myself it was okay. I needed to respect my body and give it time to rebuild and to become strong. I swam until I lost track of the laps. It felt like I was flying, gliding, and soaring across the pond as James Horner's inspirational music "Flight" played in my head.

I was regaining energy, and my life.

I rolled over onto my back and swam backstroke.

White clouds parted and the blue sky expanded. Frankie paddled next to me and I dog-paddled with her. She grinned and swam faster. She was so competitive. I had to work hard to stay at her shoulder.

Three weeks later, on July 24, I saw Dr. Rawal. He planned to check my heart before I went on the book tour to make sure I was doing fine. I wanted to ask him something out of the ordinary, but I wasn't sure how.

He listened to my heart and lungs and said I was doing fantastic. I told him I swam in upstate New York. My longest swim was forty minutes, and I felt great during and after the swim. He was so pleased.

"I've been trying to think of what else I can do to get

my heart back to normal. Could I listen to your heartbeat so I can compare it with mine and try to make mine sound more like yours?"

"Sure," he said, grinning.

I don't think he ever had a patient ask him to do this.

He put the stethoscope in his ears and the chest piece on my chest. He laughed and realized he needed to put the stethoscope in my ears and the chest piece on his chest.

He took a deep breath and let me listen to his heart. His heartbeat was loud, strong, and even. It was beautiful. I closed my eyes and memorized his heartbeat. He moved the chest piece so I could hear the different sounds within each heartbeat. I held my breath and listened and memorized it.

I looked up, and he switched the chest piece and placed it on my chest. I didn't mean to, but I said, "Shit." My heartbeat didn't sound like his. It sounded soft, murky, almost evenly paced, but it had a long way to go before it sounded like his.

I told him I was leaving in a week for the book tour and asked if he had any advice. He said to watch my salt intake. It would be difficult when I was on the road and eating out often. He told me to bring Lasix and take it if I retained water, and if I had any problems he wanted me to call him.

27

CRAWLING

Bill Lee met me at his home in Wilmette, Illinois. We swam together as teenagers, and our swim teams competed against each other. He had been a Newport Beach lifeguard, and he escorted me on my swim in the iceberg-filled waters off Greenland. He was on the boat as a rescue swimmer, ready to jump in the water in his dry suit and pull me out if I went into hypothermia.

Bill invited me to do a book signing in Chicago and swim with his friends in Lake Michigan. I was happy to do a book signing, but I wasn't ready to swim with anyone. The longest I had swum in one stretch was four strokes across a pond. That wasn't real swimming. Lake Michigan was so large that it had a tide of up to one inch. It would have waves, currents, and cold water if the wind was blowing. It was beyond my reach. I didn't have time to build up to it. My body was recovering, but not that fast.

We spoke a few times on the phone to coordinate the book signing, and each time we talked, Bill told me he wanted me to swim with him and his friends. I told him about my heart, and that I was a lot better but I was out of shape. My speed was less than half what it had been. I was back in the water, but I was weak and slow, and it wouldn't be fun to be left behind. I had worked so hard to reach an elite level in the sport, and I had to let that go.

Bill said to just come and swim, and enjoy the water.

Lake Michigan was the color of blue diamonds, and sunlight reflected off the edges of the waves and made it sparkle. It flowed from one horizon to the other.

Bill's friends, two men and two women, jogged into the water. They dove under the waves, floated, adjusted their caps and goggles, and began sprinting toward a distant pier. Their arm strokes were fast, long, and strong, and their flutter kicks were even faster. They were four hundred meters ahead of Bill and me before we started swimming.

They were fast swimmers. I tried not to let it bother me that we were so far behind. When I was a teenager and we moved from New Hampshire to California I started training with Don Gambril, the Olympic coach. I was one of the slowest swimmers in the pool and almost always finished last. I had worked hard for many years so I wouldn't be last. It bothered me then and it bothered me now.

I watched their bodies become smaller, until all I saw were splashes. They were more than six hundred meters ahead of us.

Bill waited for me to put on my cap and goggles. He breaststroked beside me until I caught my breath. He said the water was beautiful. He loved swimming in the open water. It was wonderful to be swimming with him, but I wanted to swim close to shore.

I watched him swim beside me. There was something special about swimming together. It was like playing music together or singing together, or being on the same wavelength. You flowed through the water side by side like dolphins. I watched silvery bubbles flow out of his mouth, matched my stroke with his, and shared beautiful sights below and above the water.

Bill swam at my pace. He looked beautiful, efficient, strong, and balanced as his body moved through the water. He was lean and floating low. If he swam at his normal pace, he would have been swimming higher in the water, and more efficiently.

My arms were weak and ached after swimming two hundred meters. I didn't have the energy or the endurance to increase my pace. I used to be able to increase my speed, and my last miles would be faster than the first. It was hard to be so slow. I knew I had to be careful not to undo the gains I had made, but I wanted to swim faster. I decided to try to swim faster for a minute.

Bill felt me increase my speed, and he increased his, and smiled. He thought I had found a second gear, but I only had one speed: slow.

I had to tell myself, It's okay. Respect your body. Eight months ago you were almost dead. You're crawling back. You've come a long way. You've got a long way to go.

You'll be okay. You did okay. Be happy. Be happy to be here. Be happy you could swim with Bill. Be happy you are alive. I am happy and I am grateful.

The four swimmers reached shore long before we did. But I loved swimming with Bill. I checked my watch when we climbed out of the lake. We swam for almost an hour. I told him it was the longest swim I had done since my illness.

Bill said, "I had no idea. I hope I didn't push you too hard."

"You didn't, Bill. Sometimes I get discouraged because I am so slow. It feels like I have to start all over again, but I guess that gives me the chance to learn something new."

I had been given extra time to live. I had figured out that the most important thing was to spend more time with the people I loved. Life didn't have to be lived in a blur; it could be slowed down and enjoyed more.

Signing books that evening in Chicago was great. I loved seeing old friends and meeting new ones. The next afternoon I flew to New York City. I couldn't wait to see Sophie French. She lived on Long Island and helped arrange a venue to sign my books. We had met five years before at the New Yorker Festival. She came to listen to a panel I was on and waited so we could talk. She wanted to learn to swim, but she was afraid of the water. She asked what I advised, and I suggested that she talk with swimming coaches and find the most patient swimming instructor who knew how to adjust his or her teaching to her. Give herself time to learn and build confidence. Sometimes it takes a while to overcome fear.

Sophie learned how to swim in the pool, and she found a great coach who helped her start swimming in the ocean. She asked me when I visited if we could swim in Long Island Sound.

We swam in the Sound in the late afternoon. The water was gray blue and choppy.

When we walked into the water, and the cold waves splashed us, we laughed and giggled like two little girls. We breaststroked with our heads above water, and talked, and stood up and touched the bottom, and dolphined through the water.

Sophie didn't know how to bodysurf, so I showed her how; she caught her first wave and it lifted her legs above her head and pushed her to shore. The lacy wave broke around her and she shouted and laughed, and we rode wave after wave. There was no pressure to swim fast or far. We just had fun.

When we climbed out of the Sound, the strong wind blew the water off our bodies. We watched sailboats with large billowing sails race across the whitecapped Sound. Sophie said our swim together was a dream come true, and I said it was for me too.

Friends met me in New York City, Maryland, Washington, D.C., and Virginia. Joe met me at the Miami airport. It was so good to see him after so many conversations and so much time. He looked fit and happy, but he was walking with a limp.

He said I looked good, better than he thought I would.

It was hot and humid and it felt like I was walking in a Jacuzzi wearing my clothes.

Joe lifted my bag with one hand and placed it in the back of his truck.

We climbed into the truck; it was an instant oasis. The air conditioner was turned on high. I relaxed and breathed easier in the cool.

Joe asked me why I was wearing a jacket.

I didn't want to tell him. It would have sounded dumb. I told him it was made from light fishnet fabric.

"You look hot. It would be smart to take it off," he said.

He handed me a chilled water bottle and started to drive.

I held the water on my neck to cool the carotid artery and to cool my body and then took a long drink. Cold water always tasted good, but even better in the heat.

Joe looked at me like he was trying to figure me out, like I was a puzzle.

"Why don't you lose the jacket? You're going to get hyperthermia. You're going to overheat." He shook his head.

I told him my arms were flabby. All the muscles were gone. They looked awful. I didn't want him to see them like that.

He said no one cared. It was Miami. People walked around in light clothes and swimsuits. "You should see South Beach. Some people wear almost nothing."

I didn't think he understood the way I felt about my

arms. His arms and shoulders looked great. It looked like he had been lifting weights, but I couldn't do that.

I took the jacket off, and it was a good thing that I did. I was overheating.

He reminded me that my focus had been to get my heart back in shape, but he thought I could also get my arms back in shape. He knew Dr. Rawal didn't want me to lift heavy weights because that would put pressure on the heart, but why not lift light weights?

Maybe I could lift light weights and use multiple repetitions to rebuild my muscles.

He suggested talking with Dr. Teri Engelberg, a friend of mine who was a neurologist, who worked out daily and had studied exercise physiology.

It seemed that I always learned the most from the most uncomfortable situations.

I asked Joe if he was lifting weights. He said he wasn't able to. He had been injured on the job and was forced to retire earlier than he expected. The doctors he was seeing weren't helping him, so he was working on his own recovery. Suddenly I realized why he understood what was happening with me; he was on the biggest mountain climb of his life, just as I was challenged by the most difficult swim of my life.

I continued working on healing and I felt stronger. I felt like I was reborn, and for the first time in years, I was free to spend an evening in Paris, to hike the Himalayas, but now I listened to my heart, and what I wanted most was to fall in love and have a life with someone special.

28

THE HEART KNOWS

In October, Dr. Rawal's follow-up echocardiogram confirmed that my ejection fraction had continued to improve and that my heart was normal. I was feeling great and couldn't remember ever being so happy. Dr. Rawal didn't want to see me again for six months.

I was lucky. I had been given another chance at life, and I was enjoying each day, and everything more.

I was contacted about doing a segment for the Weather Channel. I told producer Shawn Efran I was out of shape. He said it didn't matter; all he needed was some B-roll and ten minutes of swimming.

Shawn was a perfectionist and I knew he would want to take more footage. When he produced a segment for *60 Minutes* about my swim to Antarctica, his film crew shot more than ninety hours of footage. I was excited about working with him again, but I was unsure of how long I could swim in cold water. I had lost my acclimatization.

I started in the shallow waters of Alamitos Bay in

Long Beach, where I had trained when I was fourteen for my first swim across the Catalina Channel. As I swam I thought about the miles I had swum and the life I had lived. It felt right to be there, the bay where my channel swimming began, and the place where the next chapter of my life would begin.

Shawn Efran, and his cameraman, Adam Ravetch, met me at the boat in San Pedro, California. Adam had filmed polar bears and sharks and the underwater segment of my Antarctic swim. He had watched for aggressive leopard seals to make sure that neither of us was attacked.

We climbed on board the dive boat and sailed slowly through Los Angeles Harbor and past the breakwater. The hum from the boat's engines and the slow rocking-horse motion over the rolling waves felt familiar, like the start of our great Antarctic adventure. As I looked down into the dark, deep blue water, I felt nervous. I no longer knew what I could do.

The captain turned south and paralleled the break-water and positioned the boat so the sunlight would be on our backs. I had a choice. I could be afraid of doing things all the rest of my life or I could jump back into the water and live my life.

I took off my sweat suit, stepped onto the dive plat-form, and dove into the water. I popped to the sur-face, floated, and laughed. The water was colder than I expected, but it felt good. I looked at Shawn and Adam standing on deck putting on their wetsuits. Memories of

Antarctica and the impossible things we did flooded my mind.

"How's the water?" Adam shouted.

"It's great," I said.

Adam and Shawn grinned. We were on another great adventure.

I took a deep breath, put my face in the water, and swam fifty meters, and a surge of energy went through my body and I felt alive. I swam past Long Beach and Los Angeles Harbor, past San Pedro and Point Fermin Lighthouse. The land glowed in the morning light and the Pacific sparkled.

A school of anchovy glittered below; a sea lion glided beside me and looked at me for a few moments, inhaled, and dove. I put my face in the water and watched him swim under me. The ocean was a symphony of sounds: fish were humming, purring, hooting, and crackling, dolphins squeaking and clicking.

I turned my head and breathed.

All I wanted was to see how far I could swim. I felt fantastic.

Adam leaned over the side of the boat and said, "Swim for as long as you want. We'll film you from the deck, and then I'll get in the water with you."

The strength in my arms and body was increasing and I was elated. I could swim as far as my arms would pull me.

It felt different swimming in deep water than it did

to swim in the bay. My body felt lighter, my strokes deeper and smoother. I was able to establish a cadence that allowed me to swim with ease and delight. My body danced across the currents and bounced over the curling waves. Small silvery bubbles flowed in long streams off my arms and legs and large bubbles rolled out of my mouth.

Shawn moved to the side of the boat and said, "This is a perfect day. We're getting what we wanted. Do you think you can swim a little longer?"

"Sure, I'd be happy to," I said, and checked my watch. Time had passed fast and I had done better than I expected. I had been swimming for an hour.

Adam jumped in the water and a soundman joined him.

"This feels great," he said.

"It sure does," I said.

"Remember the underwater camera is heavy. Swim slowly so I can stay with you," he said.

"No problem," I said, and laughed.

Adam dove under the water and filmed me for a long time. Shawn asked if I could swim longer.

My fingers were turning white, like they had in Dr. Keatinge's test, but my core felt warm. The longer I swam the better I felt.

I gazed at Catalina Island floating on the Pacific Ocean in the blue haze, and I wondered if I could swim to Catalina again. My heart had healed physically and emotionally. It was strong and had almost returned to its normal shape. I could do anything I wanted, but I realized that I didn't want to swim to Catalina again. I didn't need to prove to myself that I had recovered.

I would always love the sport of swimming, always love being in the water, swimming alone or with friends. I would always swim. It gave me so much pleasure and a great life of exploration. But I was freer than I had been for most of my life, and I wanted new experiences. I yearned to share them with someone special. I hoped it wasn't too late.

29

LOVE AND LIFE

The sun was almost setting. I had more errands to run and normally would have finished them before doing anything else, but I felt I needed to drive to Seal Beach to see the sunset.

It was rush hour and no one would let me into the right lane, so I missed the turn and considered driving home, but I listened to my heart.

Parking on Main Street, I jogged toward the pier, but Michael Bronfenbrenner, an old friend, was sitting inside Walt's Wharf at a table by the bar with another man and he gestured for me to come inside.

The sky was turning periwinkle, violet, and deep blue, and the clouds were white and bright pink; the sunset was going to be spectacular. I wondered who the man was with Michael. He was attractive and well dressed, as if he had just come from work.

I walked inside and Michael introduced me to Steven, his younger brother. When Steven stood and shook my hand I decided to pass on the sunset. Steven was tall, his handshake was as strong as an athlete's, his eyes were bright blue, the color of the North Atlantic, and when he smiled, I felt my heart beat faster. There was something different, something special about him.

I asked Steven if he was in Seal Beach to visit Michael. He said partly, but he was also in town to meet with the Pacific Symphony. He was a consultant and he worked with orchestras and communities across the United States to help them build concert halls. He guided them through the process, helped them figure out how to collaborate, gain support, fund, and build a new venue or renovate an old one. It often took ten years or more to complete a music hall.

His voice was melodic, with a warm tone. He asked me if I liked music. I said I loved it and that I had been attending the Pacific Symphony's concerts and had many questions. I asked if he could answer some for me.

He seemed pleased to help me understand more about his world of music.

I told him that I sat above and behind the orchestra and watched the woodwinds and strings play. They had different sheet music and I wondered how they knew when to play their parts. None of them looked at the conductor.

Steven said that they were trained musicians—some played for the movies in Hollywood—and they were able to read their music and see when the conductor cued them to play.

It was exciting to learn more about his world. Did he

feel the vibrations of the instruments flowing through his body when he listened to the orchestra play? Was this experience like being home?

He grinned and said he enjoyed feeling the music as much as listening to it.

During one concert, I watched a solo violinist play a concerto with the orchestra. Between movements he stopped and tried to tighten the strings on his violin. He couldn't do it and handed his violin to the concertmaster, the first violinist, to tighten them.

Checking the program, I noticed that the soloist was playing a Stradivarius and wondered if he was afraid to tighten the strings too much and break the instrument.

Steven said that a Stradivarius might be worth more than ten million dollars. If the concertmaster couldn't fix the violin, he would give his violin to the soloist so he could complete his piece. It wasn't unusual for violin strings or the bow to break. The bows were made from Siberian horsetail and they were stretched and held a lot of tension.

I knew that only male Siberian horsetail was used and explained that my friend played violin with the New York Philharmonic. She said male Siberian horses were able to direct their urine away from their tails and thus their tail hair was cleaner and stronger than the females'.

Steven seemed impressed with that bit of information. Funny the things people are impressed by. I told him I loved to watch musicians play their instruments and see their intense physical movements and concentration. It seemed like they were dancing as much as playing music. And the conductor was the choreographer of the dance. It was a beautiful thing to watch.

I asked if he played an instrument. He played piano. When he was seventeen years old he was practicing six hours a day, training to become a concert pianist. I loved piano, but I'd had to choose between playing and swimming. I knew I would be a better swimmer than pianist but never lost my love of listening to music.

He said it took intense concentration, a willingness to work on a piece over and over again until it was technically right, and then he had to pour himself into the music so it became an expression of his heart and soul. I admired him for his commitment and thought that he was exceptional to have that dedication at a young age.

I asked if he still played and he said not much now. He traveled too much for his work, but he sang. He was a tenor and occasionally sang at Carnegie Hall. He loved singing and he had a large repertoire.

He asked if I knew that an ocean wave and a sound wave—a wave of music—had the same physical qualities. And I was intrigued with that, and with him. Our backgrounds were different, but there were many similarities. I was fascinated. He was a teacher, listener, and learner, and during our conversation he did not look away from me nor did I glance away from him.

The only thing that brought us back to the moment

was when Michael suggested that we go for a walk on the pier. We had been sitting at the table for a long time. The restaurant was almost empty, and it was dark outside.

When we reached the pier, the wind was blowing hard, the tide was flooding, and black waves were crashing into white spray against the pier pilings, shaking the wooden planks beneath our feet.

I was happy walking beside Steven. His footsteps were light and energetic and he seemed happy too. He didn't know much about me, and I felt grateful for that. It gave him a chance to discover more about me, at the same time that I was learning about him. He asked me about my training and I pointed out the course I swam between the pier and the Seal Beach jetty. It was where I discovered what I could do with my life. It was where I dreamed and worked toward big dreams. I looked at Steven and wondered if God or fate had guided me back to the pier to begin the next chapter of life with him. My grandfather fell in love the moment he met my grandmother. Maybe it was in my genes.

We walked beneath the glowing lights on the pier. The wind was blowing hard into our faces. He tucked his head and leaned into the wind.

Was he cold?

He shook his head. He said he loved the wind and the smell of the ocean. When he was a child he had sailed with his parents across the Atlantic on ocean liners, not cruise ships. His father was a psychology professor at Cornell University and his mother was an artist who had raised six children. Steven was the youngest, so he traveled with his parents when his father lectured at universities in Europe and other parts of the world. They had lived in the Soviet Union during the Cold War, and in Europe. He said he loved exploring the world and sailing across the ocean in a storm, and I told him I felt the same things swimming in the ocean during a storm. He laughed until he realized that I was serious. He liked that I was different and I liked that about him. I didn't want our walk to end, but he had to catch a flight.

When we hugged, I felt his heart beating fast against mine.

I hoped we would see each other again. I needed to let him know and sent him an e-mail telling him how much I enjoyed the evening and he e-mailed back and said he would be back in town in a couple of weeks with his voice coach and her husband. They were going to attend the Pacific Symphony's concert and listen to them play the music of Leonard Bernstein's works. He invited me to join them.

Shirley, my friend and landlord, had already invited me to the same concert one day earlier, and I had agreed to go with her, but I didn't want to miss the chance of seeing Steven, so I went twice.

A day before the concert Steven heard from his friends. They couldn't make the concert, but he wanted to know if we could have dinner together and then listen to the music.

At the restaurant Steven suggested that we order different entrées so we could share and have more to taste. Being with him was like being with an old friend, but this was something more.

I thought he needed to know about my heart, the stress it had been through, and that I was not as strong as I had once been.

"Are you okay now?" he asked. He looked concerned.

"My heart is better than it's ever been and I'm so happy being with you."

He smiled at me and my heart beat faster.

He said he had been through some difficult challenges too, but he was healthy and he was making big changes in his life. Sometimes you had to go through difficult things to make those changes.

We sat in Segerstrom Hall in the center of the room, where we could see the entire orchestra perform.

Throughout the performance I glanced at Steven. We were floating on sound waves.

When the orchestra played "Somewhere" from *West Side Story*, Steven took my hand as an opera singer on stage sang, *"There's a place for us. A time and place for us. Hold my hand and we're halfway there . . ."*

We looked at each other, and I realized that he was falling in love with me. And I was falling in love with him.

After the concert he asked me if I wanted to go for a glass of wine. It was late, but neither of us wanted the night to be over. While we were sipping our drinks, he gently touched my fingers. He expressed his heart through his fingers when he played the piano and my fingers expressed my heart when I captured water to swim across great seas.

He explored my hand and I explored his. I felt his strength, vitality, tenderness, and love. I didn't want to let go of his hand.

At 2:00 a.m. he walked me to my car and we said good night. He asked if I would like to meet again in a week or two, and I said I would love to. But then he changed plans and we saw each other the following evening. I was beginning to experience a part of life I had never known. I was excited, happy, and afraid. I had lived my life so much alone and wasn't sure if I could adjust to being with someone. He understood but said he wanted to be with me. We could take things one step at a time, and I said we would need to take two steps at a time. One step each—together.

The next morning I went for a walk and saw Shirley. She said that I looked so happy I glowed. She asked if I was in love with Steven. I said I thought I was, but I was afraid of opening my heart to him. Something might not work, and I was afraid that it would hurt my heart.

Shirley said that you have to seize happiness. Life goes by so fast, and if you don't, it will pass you by. You have to risk your heart or you will never have lived. Her life was rich because she risked her heart. She had loved much and she was much loved.

When Steven and I saw each other again he presented

me with a dozen bright yellow roses, with long dark shiny green leaves, arranged in a deep red vase. They were so beautiful. He said he loved flowers, that his father hiked with him in the area around Ithaca, New York, and his dad taught him the names of all the flowers. I asked him if his dad showed him lady slippers. They were delicate pink ballet-slipper-shaped flowers found deep in the forests of New England and upstate New York. His father told him that lady slippers were wild orchids. They were rare and beautiful and they should never be picked so they could be enjoyed by other people and so they could reproduce, so there would be more wild orchids.

I told him my dad walked with me through the woods and fields in New Hampshire and he told me the same thing about the lady slippers. Our fathers had shared the beauty and magic of the world with us, and we carried that in our hearts, to share with each other.

He said that in a few weeks the Concert Hall of the Ordway Center, one of the music halls he had worked on, in Saint Paul, Minnesota, was opening. He asked if I would go with him. I said yes. I loved being with him.

We flew to Minneapolis, Minnesota, in late February, and we walked around the city when the air temperature hovered around 17 degrees Fahrenheit (−8.3 degrees centigrade). Frigid wind cut through our clothes, our eyes watered, our noses turned bright red and ran, and our lips were so numb we couldn't speak, but we were happy holding hands, walking through beautiful old neighborhoods, and watching a pickup hockey game on Lake of the Isles until our toes were numb. We were constantly on the go, eager to experience new things in life together. We drove to the Minneapolis Institute of Art, warmed up, and wandered through the vast and beautiful art collection. It was exciting to realize that Steven liked the same artists I did, and those I wanted to bypass, he did too. We stopped to study the drawings by da Vinci, paintings by Rembrandt, Sargent, Bonnard, Monet, O'Keeffe, and Homer, and sculptures by Matisse and Moore. We discussed what we saw and why we liked the works and shared our perspectives. He helped me see things in the paintings I would not have seen myself.

The more I explored with Steven, the more I learned, and the more I learned about him, the more I realized I was in love with him. He was kind, considerate, open, and caring, and he was fun to be with. Because of Steven, I realized that there are different kinds of love that get you through life. There is the love of friends and family, a love that helps you endure, live, and thrive, and there is romantic love. The love I felt for him was a combination of all of them. It didn't matter where we were or what we were doing. I couldn't wait to see him or be with him. He enjoyed life and enjoyed sharing what he loved with me. I realized that I was living some of the best times of my life.

When we entered the Ordway, we were happy, but that happiness grew to elation when we entered the concert hall. The room was beautiful—the walls and ceiling were made of intricately designed wood paneling, and Steven explained that the hall itself is an instrument, and that when the Saint Paul Chamber Orchestra played and the VocalEssence Chorus sang the joyful music of Prokofiev and Beethoven we would feel beautiful music wash over us. Steven said the sound of the hall was perfect, and I thought the day was too.

We began to share our dreams. Steven asked me where I wanted to visit. I said I wanted to spend an evening in Paris, and explained why. When my mother's uncle went on his honeymoon and sailed around the world, he bought a bottle of Evening in Paris, from Paris, for my mother. Back in the 1950s it was difficult in Maine to get perfume from France. My mother was thrilled with the gift. She loved the fragrance and the cobalt-colored bottle. The perfume was gone, but I could smell a hint of the fragrance. I had asked her if she remembered when she wore it—if there were special dates or dances, and she looked sad for a moment and said she had saved the perfume for years in her dresser. One evening when she was going out with my father, she tried to spray the perfume on her wrist, but it had evaporated.

But she kept the bottle because it reminded her of her uncle and the excitement she felt when he gave her the perfume. She smiled and told me to enjoy the gifts I was given. Don't store them away for some future time because they might evaporate.

I told Steven he was the gift I had been given, and I was enjoying every day with him.

A few weeks later a package was delivered. Steven ran out to get it. He was smiling when he presented it to me.

I opened the box and inside was a bottle of Evening in Paris. I took off the lid and sprayed it on my wrist. I smelled the delicate concentrated bouquet of flowers: bergamot, violet, lilac, jasmine, rose, clover, and linden. The scent was beautiful, warm, and delicate, like my mother. I turned my wrist so Steven could smell the scent, and when he smiled his eyes lit up.

He made me feel loved. And, anytime of day he sang to me, Russian and American folk songs, and Irish chanteys his father had sung to him. He sang songs from the *Sound of Music,* music I remembered from childhood, and he sang Bach's Mass in B Minor, one of the most exalted sacred choral works I had ever heard.

Steven sang when he was happy, when he wanted to share a song, and when he wanted me to know that he loved me. I loved to hear him sing. I wanted to share what I loved with him, but he said he wasn't very comfortable in the water. He had trouble breathing. That was the most important part of swimming, I told him. He learned how to breathe differently, like a swimmer, not a singer, and then he was able to float.

It was a beautiful thing to watch him start to swim, to share what I loved with him and see him come to love it too. It was fun to be with him and share small and great adventures. And he wanted me to experience more of what he loved. He took me to see the San Francisco Ballet perform *Don Quixote*. He had been CFO for the company for seven years and explained that we were watching some of the finest ballet dancers in the world. They were world-class athletes. I was captivated by the performance. The dancers were so agile, graceful, and powerful.

We flew to New York City to watch the Royal Ballet perform Mendelssohn's *Midsummer Night's Dream,* and stayed at the Algonquin Hotel, a writers' gathering place and safe harbor. The Royal Ballet's performance was ethereal and inspired, and the dancers leaped so that they seemed to be suspended for moments in space held by the orchestra's high notes.

Steven and I became closer. Our friendship and love for each other grew deeper. He began introducing me to his close friends. We went to see Jack London's home in Sonoma, California, with Steven's voice coach Linda and her husband, Ken. We were familiar with London's books, but we were surprised by the number of displays and the depth of information about his life. We climbed to the second floor and heard a piano that Charmian, London's wife, had played. Volunteers came to the home to play music for visitors. The woman playing the piano was just finishing her program, and Steven was marveling about the sound of the piano and the different way the Steinway was constructed. I asked the woman if it would be okay if Steven played for us. She smiled and offered her seat at the bench. Steven began playing Beethoven, Bach, and Schumann. We stood in a circle and listened in awe as other people hurried up the stairs to join us and listen. It was a magical moment, and we wanted to experience many more together. We knew it in our hearts.

A NOTE ON THE TYPE

This book was set in Adobe Garamond. Designed for the Adobe Corporation by Robert Slimbach, the fonts are based on types first cut by Claude Garamond (ca. 1480–1561). Garamond was a pupil of Geoffroy Tory's and is believed to have followed the Venetian models, although he introduced a number of important differences, and it is to him that we owe the letter we now know as "old style." He gave his letters a certain elegance and feeling of movement that won their creator an immediate reputation and the patronage of Francis I of France.

Composed by North Market Street Graphics,
Lancaster, Pennsylvania

Printed and bound by R. R. Donnelley,
Harrisonburg, Virginia

Designed by M. Kristen Bearse